REMINISCENCES OF TOLSTOY, CHEKHOV AND ANDREEV

In the possession of S. S. Koteliansky

LEO TOLSTOY

From a statuette by Ginsburg, 1904,
presented to "*My dearest friend H. G. Wells, 5 · 10 · '20*"

REMINISCENCES OF

TOLSTOY, CHEKHOV
AND ANDREEV

by

Maxim Gorky

Maksim Gorkii, 1868-1936

Authorized translation from the Russian by
Katherine Mansfield, S. S. Koteliansky
and Leonard Woolf

VALPARAISO
INDIANA

THE HOGARTH PRESS
42 WILLIAM IV STREET, LONDON, W.C.2
1948

PUBLISHED BY
The Hogarth Press Ltd
LONDON

*

Clarke, Irwin & Co. Ltd
TORONTO

First published   1934
Second impression 1948

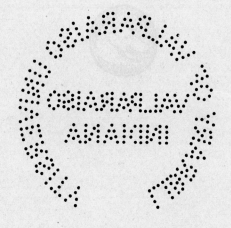

Printed in Great Britain
by Butler & Tanner Ltd., Frome and London

CONTENTS

PUBLISHER'S NOTE TO THE
FIRST EDITION

FOURTEEN years ago The Hogarth Press published Maxim Gorky's *Reminiscences of Leo Nikolaevich Tolstoy*, and it is not an exaggeration to say that it was recognized almost immediately as one of the few masterpieces of modern biography. The first edition was exhausted in a few months and the book was reprinted before the end of 1920. It has, however, been out of print for many years. Owing to continual enquiries about it, it has seemed desirable once more to reprint it, and opportunity has been taken to include with it, in a single volume, Gorky's reminiscences of the other two great Russian writers, Chekhov and Andreev. The translation of the Chekhov reminiscences was first published in 1921 together with Chekhov's Note-Books (Hogarth Press), the Andreev reminiscences in a limited edition in 1931 (Heinemann).

1934

REMINISCENCES OF
LEO NIKOLAEVICH TOLSTOY

Translated from the Russian by
S. S. KOTELIANSKY AND
LEONARD WOOLF

PREFACE

THIS little book is composed of fragmentary notes written by me during the period when I lived in Oleise and Leo Nikolaevich at Gaspra in the Crimea. They cover the period of Tolstoy's serious illness and of his subsequent recovery. The notes were carelessly jotted down on scraps of paper, and I thought I had lost them, but recently I have found some of them. Then I have also included here an unfinished letter written by me under the influence of the " going away " of Leo Nikolaevich from Yasnaya Polyana, and of his death. I publish the letter just as it was written at the time, and without correcting a single word. And I do not finish it, for somehow or other this is not possible.

M. GORKY

NOTES

I

THE thought which beyond others most often and conspicuously gnaws at him is the thought of God. At moments it seems, indeed, not to be a thought, but a violent resistance to something which he feels above him. He speaks of it less than he would like, but thinks of it always. It can scarcely be said to be a sign of old age, a presentiment of death—no, I think that it comes from his exquisite human pride, and—a bit—from a sense of humiliation: for, being Leo Tolstoy, it is humiliating to have to submit one's will to a streptococcus. If he were a scientist, he would certainly evolve the most ingenious hypotheses, make great discoveries.

II

HE has wonderful hands—not beautiful, but knotted with swollen veins, and yet full of a singular expressiveness and the power of creativeness. Probably Leonardo da Vinci had hands like that. With such hands

13

one can do anything. Sometimes, when talking, he will move his fingers, gradually close them into a fist, and then, suddenly opening them, utter a good, full-weight word. He is like a god, not a Sabaoth or Olympian, but the kind of Russian god who " sits on a maple throne under a golden lime tree," not very majestic, but perhaps more cunning than all the other gods.

III

He treats Sulerzhitski with the tenderness of a woman. For Chekhov his love is paternal—in this love is the feeling of the pride of a creator—Suler rouses in him just tenderness, a perpetual interest and rapture which never seem to weary the sorcerer. Perhaps there is something a little ridiculous in this feeling, like the love of an old maid for a parrot, a pug-dog, or a tom-cat. Suler is a fascinatingly wild bird from some strange unknown land. A hundred men like him could change the face, as well as the soul, of a provincial town. Its face they would smash and its soul they would fill with a passion for riotous, brilliant, headstrong wildness. One loves Suler easily and gaily, and when I see how carelessly women accept him, they surprise and anger me. Yet under this carelessness is hidden, perhaps, caution. Suler is not reliable. What will he do to-morrow? He may throw a bomb or he may join a troupe of public-house minstrels. He has energy enough for three lifetimes, and fire of life—so much that he seems to sweat sparks like over-heated iron

IV

GOLDENWEISER played Chopin, which called forth these remarks from Leo Nikolaevich: "A certain German princeling said: 'Where you want to have slaves, there you should have as much music as possible.' That's a true thought, a true observation—music dulls the mind. Especially do the Catholics realize that; our priests, of course, won't reconcile themselves to Mendelssohn in church. A Tula priest assured me that Christ was not a Jew, though the son of the Jewish God and his mother a Jewess—he did admit that, but says he: 'It's impossible.' I asked him: 'But how then? . . .' He shrugged his shoulders and said: 'That's just the mystery.' "

V

" AN intellectual is like the old Galician Prince Vladimirko, who, as far back as the twelfth century, ' boldly ' declared: ' There are no miracles in our

time.' Six hundred years have passed and all the
intellectuals hammer away at each other: ' There
are no miracles, there are no miracles.' And all the
people believe in miracles, just as they did in the
twelfth century."

VI

" THE minority, feel the need of God because they
have got everything else, the majority because they
have nothing."

I would put it differently: the majority believe in
God from cowardice, only the few believe in him from
fullness of soul.

VII

HE advised me to read Buddhistic scriptures. Of
Buddhism and Christ he always speaks sentimentally.
When he speaks about Christ, it is always peculiarly
poor, no enthusiasm, no feeling in his words, and no
spark of real fire. I think he regards Christ as simple
and deserving of pity, and, although at times he
admires Him, he hardly loves Him. It is as though
he were uneasy: if Christ came to a Russian village,
the girls might laugh at Him.

VIII

To-day the Grand Duke Nicolai Mikhaielovich was at Tolstoy's, evidently a very clever man. His behaviour is very modest; he talks little. He has sympathetic eyes and a fine figure, quiet gestures. Leo Nikolaevich smiled caressingly at him, and spoke now French, now English. In Russian he said:

" Karamzin wrote for the Tsar, Solovev long and tediously, and Kluchevski for his own amusement. Cunning fellow, Kluchevski: at first you get the impression that he is praising, but as you read on you see that he is blaming."

Someone mentioned Zabielin.

" He's nice. An amateur collector, he collects everything, whether it is useful or not. He describes food as if he had never had a square meal; but he is very, very amusing."

IX

He reminds me of those pilgrims who all their life long, stick in hand, walk the earth, travelling thousands of miles from one monastery to another, from one saint's relics to another, terribly homeless and alien to all men and things. The world is not for them, nor God either. They pray to Him from habit,

B

and in their secret soul they hate Him—why does He drive them over the earth, from one end to the other ? What for ? People are stumps, roots, stones on the path; one stumbles over them, and sometimes is hurt by them. One can do without them, but it is pleasant sometimes to surprise a man with one's own unlikeness to him, to show one's difference from him.

X

" FRIEDRICH of Prussia said very truly: ' Everyone must save himself in his own way.' He also said: ' Argue as much as you like, but obey.' But when dying he confessed: ' I have grown weary of ruling slaves.' So-called great men are always terribly contradictory: that is forgiven them with all their other follies. Though contradictoriness is not folly: a fool is stubborn, but does not know how to contradict himself. Yes, Friedrich was a strange man: among the Germans he won the reputation of being the best king, yet he could not bear them; he disliked even Goethe and Wieland."

XI

" ROMANTICISM comes from the fear of looking straight into the eyes of truth," he said yesterday with regard to Balmont's poems. Suler disagreed with him and, lisping with excitement, read very feelingly some more poems.

" These, Liovushka, are not poems; they are charlatanism, rubbish, as people said in the Middle Ages, a nonsensical stringing together of words. Poetry is art-less; when Fet wrote:

> I know not myself what I will sing,
> But only my song is ripening,

he expressed a genuine, real, people's sense of poetry. The peasant, too, doesn't know that he's a poet—oh, oi, ah, and aye—and there comes off a real song, straight from the soul, like a bird's. These new poets of yours are inventing. There are certain silly French things called *articles de Paris*—well, that's what your stringers of verses produce. Nekrasov's miserable verses, too, are invented from beginning to end."

" And Béranger ? " Suler asked.

" Béranger—that's quite different. What's there in common between the French and us ? They are sensualists; the life of the spirit is not as important to them as the flesh. To a Frenchman woman is everything. They are a worn-out, emasculated people. Doctors say that all consumptives are sensualists."

Suler began to argue with his peculiar directness, pouring out a random flood of words. Leo Nikolaevich looked at him and said with a broad smile:

" You are peevish to-day, like a girl who has reached the age when she should marry but has no lover."

XII

THE illness dried him up still more, burnt something out of him. Inwardly he seemed to become lighter, more transparent, more resigned. His eyes are still keener, his glance piercing. He listens attentively as though recalling something which he has forgotten or as though waiting for something new and unknown. In Yasnaya Polyana he seemed to me a man who knew everything and had nothing more to learn—a man who had settled every question.

XIII

IF he were a fish, he would certainly swim only in the ocean, never coming to the narrow seas, and particularly not to the flat waters of earthly rivers. Around him here there rest or dart hither and thither the little fishes: what he says does not interest them, is not necessary to them, and his silence does not frighten or move them. Yet his silence is impressive, like that of a real hermit driven out from this world. Though he speaks a great deal and as a duty upon certain subjects, his silence is felt to be still greater. Certain things one cannot tell to anyone. Surely he has some thoughts of which he is afraid.

XIV

SOMEONE sent him an excellent version of the story of Christ's godson. He read it aloud with pleasure to Suler, Chekhov—he read amazingly well. He was especially amused by the devils torturing the land-owners. There was something which I did not like in that. He cannot be insincere, but, if this be sincere, then it makes it worse.

Then he said:

" How well the peasants compose stories. Everything is simple, the words few, and a great deal of feeling. Real wisdom uses few words; for instance, ' God have mercy on us.' "

Yet the story is a cruel one.

XV

HIS interest in me is ethnological. In his eyes I belong to a species not familiar to him—only that.

XVI

I READ my story *The Bull* to him. He laughed much, and praised my knowledge of " the tricks of the language."

" But your treatment of words is not skilful; all your peasants speak cleverly. In actual life what they say is silly and incoherent, and at first you cannot make out what a peasant wants to say. That is done deliberately; under the silliness of their words is always concealed a desire to allow the other person to show what is in his mind. A good peasant will never show at once what is in his own mind: it is not profitable. He knows that people approach a stupid man frankly and directly, and that's the very thing he wants. You stand revealed before him and he at once sees all your weak points. He is suspicious, he is afraid to tell his inmost thoughts even to his wife. But with your peasants in every story everything is revealed: it's a universal counsel of wisdom. And they all speak in aphorisms; that's not true to life, either; aphorisms are not natural to the Russian language."

" What about sayings and proverbs ? "

" That's a different thing. They are not of to-day's manufacture."

" But you yourself often speak in aphorisms."

"Never. There again you touch everything up; people as well as Nature—especially people. So did Lyeskov, an affected, finicking writer whom nobody reads now. Don't let anyone influence you, fear no one, and then you'll be all right."

XVII

In his diary which he gave me to read, I was struck by a strange aphorism: "God is my desire."

To-day, on returning him the book, I asked him what it meant.

"An unfinished thought," he said, glancing at the page and screwing up his eyes. "I must have wanted to say: 'God is my desire to know Him.' . . . No, not that. . . ." He began to laugh, and, rolling up the book into a tube, he put it into the big pocket of his blouse. With God he has very suspicious relations; they sometimes remind me of the relation of "two bears in one den."

XVIII

On science.

"Science is a bar of gold made by a charlatan alchemist. You want to simplify it, to make it accessible to all: you find that you have coined a lot

of false coins. When the people realize the real value
of those coins, they won't thank you."

XIX

WE walked in the Yusopov Park. He spoke superbly
about the customs of the Moscow aristocracy. A big
Russian peasant woman was working on the flower-
bed, bent at right angles, showing her ivory legs,
shaking her ten-pound breasts. He looked at her
attentively.

" It is those caryatids who have kept all that
magnificence and extravagance going. Not only by
the labour of peasant men and women, not only by the
taxes they pay, but in the literal sense by their blood.
If the aristocracy had not from time to time mated
with such horse-women as she, they would have died
out long ago. It is impossible with impunity to waste
one's strength, as the young men of my time did. But
after sowing their wild oats, many married serf-girls
and produced a good breed. In that way, too, the
peasant's strength saved them. That strength is
everywhere in place. Half the aristocracy always has
to spend its strength on itself, and the other half to
dilute itself with peasant blood and thus diffuse the
peasant blood a little. It's useful."

XX

Of women he talks readily and much, like a French novelist, but always with the coarseness of a Russian peasant. Formerly it used to affect me unpleasantly. To-day in the Almond Park he asked Anton Chekhov:

"You whored a great deal when you were young?"

Anton Pavlovich, with a confused smile, and pulling at his little beard, muttered something inaudible, and Leo Nikolaevich, looking at the sea, confessed:

"I was an indefatigable. . . ."

He said this penitently, using at the end of the sentence a salty peasant word. And I noticed for the first time how simply he used the word, as though he knew no more fitting one to use. All those kinds of words, coming from his shaggy lips, sound simple and natural and lose their soldierly coarseness and filth. I remember my first meeting with him and his talk about *Varenka Oliessova* and *Twenty-six and One.* From the ordinary point of view what he said was a string of indecent words. I was perplexed by it and even offended. I thought that he considered me incapable of understanding any other kind of language. I understand now: it was silly to have felt offended.

XXI

HE sat on the stone bench in the shade of the cypresses, looking very lean, small and grey, and yet resembling Sabaoth, who is a little tired and is amusing himself by trying to whistle in tune with a chaffinch. The bird sang in the darkness of the thick foliage: he peered up at it, screwing up his sharp little eyes, and, pursing his lips like a child, he whistled incompetently.

" What a furious little creature. It's in a rage. What bird is it ? "

I told him about the chaffinch and its characteristic jealousy.

" All life long one song," he said, " and yet jealous. Man has a thousand songs in his heart and is yet blamed for jealousy; is it fair ? " He spoke musingly, as though asking himself questions. " There are moments when a man says to a woman more than she ought to know about him. He speaks and forgets, but she remembers. Perhaps jealousy comes from the fear of degrading one's soul, of being humiliated and ridiculous ? Not that a woman is dangerous who holds a man by his . . . but she who holds him by his soul. . . ."

When I pointed out the contradiction in this with his *Kreutzer Sonata*, the radiance of a sudden smile beamed through his beard, and he said:

" I am not a chaffinch."

In the evening, while walking, he suddenly said: " Man survives earthquakes, epidemics, the horrors of disease, and all the agonies of the soul, but for all time his most tormenting tragedy has been, is, and will be—the tragedy of the bedroom."

Saying this, he smiled triumphantly: at times he has the broad, calm smile of a man who has overcome something extremely difficult or from whom some sharp, long-gnawing pain has lifted suddenly. Every thought burrows into his soul like a tick; he either tears it out at once or allows it to have its fill of his blood, and then, when full, it just drops off of itself.

. . . . . .

He read to Suler and me a variant of the scene of the fall of " Father Sergius "—a merciless scene. Suler pouted and fidgeted uneasily.

" What's the matter ? Don't you like it ? " Leo Nikolaevich asked.

" It's too brutal, as though from Dostoevsky. She is a filthy girl, and her breasts like pancakes, and all that. Why didn't he sin with a beautiful healthy woman ? "

" That would be sin without justification; as it is, there is justification in pity for the girl. Who could desire her as she is ? "

" I cannot make it out. . . ."

" There's a great deal, Liovushka, which you can't make out: you're not shrewd. . . ."

There came in Andrei Lvovich's wife, and the conversation was interrupted. As she and Suler went out, Leo Nikolaevich said to me: " Leopold is the purest man I know. He is like that: if he did something bad, it would be out of pity for someone."

XXII

HE talks most of God, of peasants, and of woman; of literature rarely and little, as though literature were something alien to him. Woman, in my opinion, he regards with implacable hostility and loves to punish her, unless she be a Kittie or Natasha Rostov, i.e. a creature not too narrow. It is the hostility of the male who has not succeeded in getting all the pleasure he could, or it is the hostility of spirit against " the degrading impulses of the flesh." But it is hostility, and cold, as in *Anna Karenin*. Of " the degrading impulses of the flesh " he spoke well on Sunday in a conversation with Chekhov and Yelpatievski about Rousseau's *Confessions*. Suler wrote down what he said, and later, while preparing coffee, burnt it in the spirit-lamp. Once before he burnt Leo Nikolaevich's opinions on Ibsen, and he also lost the notes of the

conversation in which Leo Nikolaevich said very
pagan things on the symbolism of the marriage
ritual, agreeing to a certain extent with V. V.
Rozanov.

XXIII

IN the morning some " stundists " came to Tolstoy
from Feodosia, and to-day all day long he spoke about
peasants with rapture.

At lunch: " They came both so strong and fleshy;
says one: ' Well, we've come uninvited,' and the
other says: ' With God's help we shall leave un-
beaten,' " and he broke out into childlike laughter,
shaking all over.

After lunch, on the terrace:

" We shall soon cease completely to understand the
language of the people. Now we say: ' The theory of
progress,' ' the role of the individual in history,' ' the
evolution of science '; and a peasant says: ' You
can't hide an awl in a sack,' and all theories, histories,
evolutions become pitiable and ridiculous, because
they are incomprehensible and unnecessary to the
people. But the peasant is stronger than we; he is
more tenacious of life, and there may happen to us
what happened to the tribe of Atzurs, of whom it was
reported to a scholar: ' All the Atzurs have died out,

but there is a parrot here who knows a few words of
their language.' "

XXIV

" WITH her body woman is more sincere than man,
but with her mind she lies. And when she lies, she
does not believe herself ; but Rousseau lied and
believed his lies."

XXV

" DOSTOEVSKY described one of his mad characters
as living and taking vengeance on himself and others
because he had served a cause in which he did not
believe. He wrote that about himself ; that is, he
could have said the same of himself."

XXVI

" SOME of the words used in church are amazingly
obscure: what meaning is there, for instance, in the
words: ' The earth is God's and the fulness thereof ' ?
That is not Holy Scripture, but a kind of popular
scientific materialism."

" But you explained the words somewhere," said
Suler.

" Many things are explained. . . .   An explanation does not go up to the hilt.' "

And he gave a cunning little smile.

XXVII

He likes putting difficult and malicious questions:
  What do you think of yourself ?
  Do you love your wife ?
  Do you think my son, Leo, has talent ?
  How do you like Sophie Andreevna ?[1]
  Once he asked: " Are you fond of me, Alexei
Maximovich ? "

This is the maliciousness of a " bogatyr "[2]: Vaska
Buslaev played such pranks in his youth, mischievous
fellow. He is experimenting, all the time testing
something, as if he were going to fight. It is interesting, but not much to my liking. He is the devil,
and I am still a babe, and he should leave me alone.

XXVIII

Perhaps peasant to him means merely—bad smell.
He always feels it, and involuntarily has to talk of it.

[1] Tolstoy's wife.

[2] A hero in Russian legend, brave, but wild and self-willed like
a child.

Last night I told him of my battle with General Kornet's widow; he laughed until he cried, and he got a pain in his side and groaned and kept on crying out in a thin scream:

" With the shovel! On the bottom with the shovel, eh ? Right on the bottom! Was it a broad shovel ? "

Then, after a pause, he said seriously: " It was generous in you to strike her like that; any other man would have struck her on the head for that. Very generous! You understood that she wanted you ? "

" I don't remember. I hardly think that I can have understood."

" Well now! But it's obvious. Of course she wanted you."

" I did not live for that then."

" Whatever you may live for, it's all the same. You are evidently not much of a lady's man. Anyone else in your place would have made his fortune out of the situation, would have become a landed proprietor and have ended by making one of a pair of drunkards."

After a silence: " You are funny—don't be offended—very funny. And it's very strange that you should still be good-natured when you might well be spiteful. . . . Yes, you might well be spiteful. . . . You're strong .. . . that's good. . . ."

And after another silence, he added thoughtfully:

" Your mind I don't understand—it's a very tangled mind—but your heart is sensible . . . yes, a sensible heart."

NOTE.—When I lived in Kazan, I entered the service of General Kornet's wife as doorkeeper and gardener. She was a Frenchwoman, a general's widow, a young woman, fat, and with the tiny feet of a little girl. Her eyes were amazingly beautiful, restless and always greedily alert. Before her marriage she was, I think, a huckstress or a cook or, possibly, even a woman of the town. She would get drunk early in the morning and come out in the yard or garden dressed only in a chemise with an orange-coloured gown over it, in Tartar slippers made of red morocco, and on her head a mane of thick hair. Her hair, carelessly done, hung about her red cheeks and shoulders. A young witch! She used to walk about the garden, humming French songs and watching me work, and every now and then she would go to the kitchen window and call:

" Pauline, give me something."

" Something " always meant the same thing—a glass of wine with ice in it.

In the basement of her house there lived three young ladies, the Princesses D. G., whose mother was dead and whose father, a Commissariat-General, had gone off elsewhere. General Kornet's widow

C

took a dislike to the girls and tried to get rid of them
by doing every kind of offensive thing to them. She
spoke Russian badly, but swore superbly, like an
expert drayman. I very much disliked her attitude
towards these harmless girls—they looked so sad,
frightened, and defenceless. One afternoon, two of
them were walking in the garden when suddenly the
General's widow appeared, drunk as usual, and began
to shout at them to drive them out of the garden.
They began walking silently away, but the General's
widow stood in the gateway, completely blocking it
with her body like a cork, and started swearing at
them and using Russian words like a regular drayman.
I asked her to stop swearing and let the girls go out,
but she shouted:

" You, I know you! You get through their window
at night."

I was angry, and, taking her by the shoulders,
pushed her away from the gate; but she broke away,
and, facing me, quickly undid her dress, lifted up
her chemise, and shouted:

" I'm nicer than those rats."

Then I lost my temper. I took her by the neck,
turned her round, and struck her with my shovel
below the back, so that she skipped out of the gate
and ran across the yard, crying out three times in
great surprise: " O! O! O! "

After that, I got my passport from her confidante, Pauline—also a drunken but very wily woman—took my bundle under my arm, and left the place; and the General's widow, standing at the window with a red shawl in her hand, shouted:

" I won't call the police—it's all right—listen—come back—don't be afraid."

XXIX

I ASKED him: " Do you agree with Pozdnishev[1] when he says that doctors have destroyed and are destroying thousands and hundreds of thousands of people ? "

" Are you very interested to know ? "

" Very."

" Then I shan't tell you."

And he smiled, playing with his thumbs.

I remember in one of his stories he makes a comparison between a quack village vet. and a doctor of medicine:

" The words ' giltchak,' ' potchetchny,' ' blood-letting,'[2] are they not precisely the same as nerves, rheumatism, organisms, etc. ? "

And this was written after Jenner, Behring, Pasteur. It is perversity!

[1] In *Kreutzer Sonata*.

[2] Words used by quack vets. for the diseases of horses.

XXX

How strange that he is so fond of playing cards. He plays seriously, passionately. His hands become nervous when he takes the cards up, exactly as if he were holding live birds instead of inanimate pieces of cardboard.

XXXI

" DICKENS said a very clever thing: ' Life is given to us on the definite understanding that we boldly defend it to the last.' On the whole, he was a sentimental, loquacious, and not very clever writer, but he knew how to construct a novel as no one else could, certainly better than Balzac. Someone has said: ' Many are possessed by the passion for writing books, but few are ashamed of them afterwards.' Balzac was not ashamed, nor was Dickens, and both of them wrote quite a number of bad books. Still, Balzac is a genius. Or at any rate the thing which you can only call genius. . . ."

XXXII

SOMETIMES he seems to be conceited and intolerant, like a Volga preacher, and this is terrible in a man who is the sounding-bell of this world. Yesterday he said to me:

" I am more of a mouzhik than you and I feel better in a mouzhik way."

God, he ought not to boast of it, he must not!

XXXIII

I READ him some scenes from my play, *The Lower Depths*; he listened attentively, and then asked:

" Why do you write that ? "

I explained as best I could.

" One always notices that you jump like a cock on to everything. And more—you always want to paint all the grooves and cracks over with your own paint. You remember that Andersen says: ' The gilt will come off and the pig-skin will remain '; just as our peasants say: ' Everything will pass away, the truth alone will remain.' You'd much better not put the plaster on, for you yourself will suffer for it later. Again, your language is very skilful, with all kinds of tricks—that's no good. You ought to write more simply; people speak simply, even incoherently, and that's good. A peasant doesn't ask: ' Why is a third more than a fourth, if four is always more than three,' as one learned young lady asked. No tricks, please."

He spoke irritably; clearly he disliked very much

what I had read to him. And after a silence, looking over my head, he said gloomily:

" Your old man is not sympathetic, one does not believe in his goodness. The actor is all right, he's good. You know *Fruits of Enlightenment*? My cook there is rather like your actor. Writing plays is difficult. But your prostitute also came off well, they must be like that. Have you known many of them ? "

" I used to."

" Yes, one can see that. Truth always shows itself. Most of what you say comes out of yourself, and therefore you have no characters, and all your people have the same face. I should think you don't understand women; they don't come off with you. One does not remember them. . . ."

At this moment A. L.'s wife came in and called us to come to tea, and he got up and went out very quickly, as if he were glad to end the conversation.

XXXIV

" WHAT is the most terrible dream you have ever had ? " Tolstoy asked me.

I rarely have dreams and remember them badly, but two have remained in my memory and probably will for the rest of my life.

I dreamt once that I saw the sky scrofulous, putrescent, greenish-yellow, and the stars in it were round, flat, without rays, without lustre, like scabs on the skin of a diseased person. And there glided across this putrescent sky slowly reddish forked lightning, rather like a snake, and when it touched a star the star swelled up into a ball and burst noise-lessly, leaving behind it a darkish spot, like a little smoke; and then the spot vanished quickly in the bleared and liquid sky. Thus all the stars one after another burst and perished, and the sky, growing darker and more horrible, at last whirled upwards, bubbled, and, bursting into fragments, began to fall on my head in a kind of cold jelly, and in the spaces between the fragments there appeared a shiny black-ness as though of iron. Leo Nikolaevich said: " Now that comes from a learned book; you must have read something on astronomy; hence the nightmare. And the other dream ? "

The other dream: a snowy plain, smooth like a sheet of paper; no hillock, no tree, no bush anywhere, only—barely visible—a few rods poked out from under the snow. And across the snow of this dead desert from horizon to horizon there stretched a yellow strip of a hardly distinguishable road, and over the road there marched slowly a pair of grey felt top-boots— empty.

He raised his shaggy, werewolf eyebrows, looked at me intently and thought for a while.

" That's terrible. Did you really dream that ?—you didn't invent it ? But there's something bookish in it also."

And suddenly he got angry, and said, irritably, sternly, rapping his knee with his finger: " But you're not a drinking man ? It's unlikely that you ever drank much. And yet there's something drunken in these dreams. There was a German writer, Hoffmann, who dreamt that card tables ran about the street, and all that sort of thing, but then he was a drunkard—a ' calaholic,' as our literate coachmen say. Empty boots marching—that's really terrible. Even if you did invent it, it's good. Terrible."

Suddenly he gave a broad smile, so that even his cheek-bones beamed.

" And imagine this: suddenly, in the Tverskaya Street, there runs a card table with its curved legs, its boards clap, clap, raising a chalky dust, and you can even still see the numbers on the green cloth— excise clerks playing whist on it for three days and nights on end—the table could not bear it any longer and ran away.

He laughed, and then, probably noticing that I was a little hurt by his distrust of me:

" Are you hurt because I thought your dreams

bookish ? Don't be annoyed; sometimes, I know, one invents something without being aware of it, something which one cannot believe, which can't possibly be believed, and then one imagines that one dreamt it and did not invent it at all. There was a story which an old landowner told. He dreamt that he was walking in a wood and came out of it on to a steppe. On the steppe he saw two hills, which suddenly turned into a woman's breasts, and between them rose up a black face, which, instead of eyes, had two moons like white spots. The old man dreamt that he was standing between the woman's legs, in front of him a deep, dark ravine, which sucked him in. After the dream his hair began to grow grey and his hands to tremble, and he went abroad to Doctor Kneip to take a water cure. But, really, he must have seen something of the kind—he was a dissolute fellow."

He patted me on the shoulder.

" But you are neither a drunkard nor dissolute— how do you come to have such dreams ? "

" I don't know."

" We know nothing about ourselves."

He sighed, screwed up his eyes, thought for a bit, and then added in a low voice: " We know nothing."

This evening, during our walk, he took my arm and said:

" The boots are marching—terrible, eh ? Quite empty—tiop, tiop—and the snow scrunching. Yes, it's good; but you are very bookish, very. Don't be cross, but it's bad and will stand in your way."

I am scarcely more bookish than he, and at the time I thought him a cruel rationalist despite all his pleasant little phrases.

XXXV

At times he gives one the impression of having just arrived from some distant country, where people think and feel differently and their relations and language are different. He sits in a corner tired and grey, as though the dust of another earth were on him, and he looks attentively at everything with the look of a foreigner or of a dumb man.

Yesterday, before dinner, he came into the drawing-room, just like that, his thoughts far away. He sat down on the sofa, and, after a moment's silence, suddenly said, swaying his body a little, rubbing the palm of his hand on his knee, and wrinkling up his face :

" Still, that is not all—not all."

Someone, always stolidly stupid as a flat-iron, asked : " What do you say ? "

He looked at him fixedly, and then, bending forward and looking on the terrace where I was

sitting with Doctor Nikitin and Yelpatievski, he said:
" What are you talking about ? "

" Plehve."

" Plehve . . . Plehve . . ." he repeated musingly
after a pause, as though he heard the name for the
first time. Then he shook himself like a bird, and
said, with a faint smile:

" To-day from early morning I have had a silly
thing running in my head; someone once told me
that he saw the following epitaph in a cemetery:

> Beneath this stone there rests Ivan Yegoryev;
> A tanner by trade, he always wetted hides.
> His work was honest, his heart good, but, behold,
> He passed away, leaving his business to his wife.
> He was not yet old and might still have done a lot of
>   work,
> But God took him away to the life of paradise on the
>   night
> Friday to Saturday in Passion week . . .

and something like that. . . ." He was silent, and
then, nodding his head and smiling faintly, added:
" In human stupidity, when it is not malicious,
there is something very touching, even beautiful.
. . . There always is."

They called us to come to dinner.

XXXVI

" I DO not like people when they are drunk, but I
know some who become interesting when they are

tipsy, who acquire what is not natural to them in their sober state—wit, beauty of thought, alertness, and richness of language. In such cases I am ready to bless wine.".

Suler tells how he was once walking with Leo Nikolaevich in Tverskaya Street when Tolstoy noticed in the distance two soldiers of the Guards. The metal of their accoutrements shone in the sun; their spurs jingled; they kept step like one man; their faces, too, shone with the self-assurance of strength and youth.

Tolstoy began to grumble at them: " What pompous stupidity! Like animals trained by the whip. . . ."

But when the Guardsmen came abreast with him, he stopped, followed them caressingly with his eyes, and said enthusiastically: " How handsome! Old Romans, eh, Liovushka ? Their strength and beauty! O Lord! How charming it is when man is handsome, how very charming! "

A LETTER

I HAVE just posted a letter to you—telegrams have arrived telling of " Tolstoy's flight," and now once more one with you in thought I write again.

Probably all I want to say about the news will seem to you confused, perhaps even harsh and ill-tempered, but you will forgive me—I am feeling as though I had been gripped by the throat and was being strangled.

I had many long conversations with him; when he was living at Gaspra in the Crimea, I often went to him and he liked coming to me; I have studied his books lovingly; it seems to me that I have the right to say what I think of him, even if it be bold and differ widely from the general opinion. I know as well as others that no man is more worthy than he of the name of genius; more complicated, contradictory, and great in everything—yes, yes, in everything. Great—in some curious sense wide, indefinable by words—there is something in him which made me desire to cry aloud to everyone: " Look what a wonderful man is living on the earth." For he is, so to say, universally and above all a man, a man of mankind.

But what always repelled me in him was that stubborn despotic inclination to turn the life of Count Leo Nikolaevich Tolstoy into " the saintly life of our blessed father, boyard Leo." As you know, he has for long intended to suffer; he expressed his regret to E. Solovyov, to Suler, that he had not succeeded, but he wanted to suffer simply, not out of a natural desire to test the resistance of his will, but with the obvious and, I repeat, the despotic intention of increasing the influence of his religious ideas, the weight of his teaching, in order to make his preaching irresistible, to make it holy in the eyes of man through his suffering, to force them to accept it; you understand, to force them. For he realizes that that preaching is not sufficiently convincing; in his diary you will, some day, read good instances of scepticism applied by him to his own preaching and personality. He knows that " martyrs and sufferers, with rare exceptions, are despots and tyrants "—he knows everything! And yet he says to himself, " Were I to suffer for my ideas they would have a greater influence." This in him always repelled me, for I cannot help feeling that it is an attempt to use violence to me—a desire to get hold of my conscience, to dazzle it with the glory of righteous blood, to put on my neck the yoke of a dogma.

He always greatly exalted immortality on the other side of life, but he preferred it on this side. A writer, national in the truest and most complete sense, he embodied in his great soul all the defects of his nation, all the mutilations caused us by the ordeals of our history; his misty preaching of " non-activity," of " non-resistance to evil "—the doctrine of passivism —this is all the unhealthy ferment of the old Russian blood, envenomed by Mongolian fatalism and almost chemically hostile to the West with its untiring creative labour, with its active and indomitable

resistance to the evil of life. What is called Tolstoy's
" anarchism," essentially and fundamentally, expresses
our Slav anti-stateism, which, again, is really a
national characteristic and desire, ingrained in our
flesh from old times, to scatter nomadically. Up to
now we have indulged that desire passionately, as you
and everyone else know. We Russians know it, too,
but we break away, always along the line of least
resistance; we see that this is pernicious, but still we
crawl farther and farther away from one another—
and these mournful cockroach journeyings are called
" the history of Russia," of a State which has been
established almost incidentally, mechanically, to the
surprise of the majority of its honest-minded citizens,
by the forces of the Variags, Tartars, Baltic Germans,
and petty constables. To their surprise, because all
the time " scattering," and only when we reached
places beyond which we could find nothing worse—
for we could go no farther—well, then we stopped and
settled down. This is the lot, the destiny to which we
are doomed—to settle in the snows and marshes by
the side of the wild Erza, Tchood, Merey, Vess, and
Muroma. Yet men arose who realized that light
must come to us not from the East but from the
West; and now he, the crown of our ancient history,
wishes, consciously or unconsciously, to stretch himself like a vast mountain across our nation's path to

Europe, to the active life which sternly demands of man the supreme effort of his spiritual forces. His attitude towards science is, too, certainly national: one sees magnificently reflected in him the old Russian village scepticism which comes from ignorance. Everything is national in him, and all his preaching is a reaction from the past, an atavism which we had already begun to shake off and overcome.

Think of his letter, " The Intelligentsia, the State, the People," written in 1905—what a pernicious, malignant thing it is! You can hear in it the sectarian's " I told you so." At the time I wrote an answer to him, based on his own words to me that he had long since forfeited the right to speak of and on behalf of the Russian people, for I am a witness of his lack of desire to listen to and understand the people who came to talk to him soul to soul. My letter was bitter, and in the end I did not send it to him.

Well, now he is probably making his last assault in order to give to his ideas the highest possible significance. Like Vasili Buslaev, he usually loved these assaults, but always so that he might assert his holiness and obtain a halo. That is dictatorial, although his teaching is justified by the ancient history of Russia and by his own sufferings of genius. Holiness is attained by flirting with sin, by subduing the will to live. People do desire to live, but he tries to persuade them: " That's all nonsense, our earthly life." It is very easy to persuade a Russian of this; he is a lazy creature who loves beyond anything else to find an excuse for his own inactivity. On the whole, of course, a Russian is not a Platon Karataev, nor an Akim, nor a Bezoukhy, nor a Neklyudov; all these men were created by history and Nature, not exactly on Tolstoy's pattern, he only improved on them in order more thoroughly to support his teaching. But, undeniably, Russia as a whole is—Tyulin above and Oblomov below. For the Tyulin above look at the year 1905, and for the Oblomov below look at Count A. N. Tolstoy, I. Bunin, look at everything round about you. Beasts and swindlers—we can leave them out of consideration, though our beast is exceedingly national—what a filthy coward he is for all his cruelty. Swindlers, of course, are international.

In Leo Nikolaevich there is much which at times roused in me a feeling very like hatred, and this hatred fell upon my soul with crushing weight. His disproportionately overgrown individuality is a monstrous phenomenon, almost ugly, and there is in him something of Svyatogor, the bogatyr, whom the earth can't hold. Yes, he *is* great. I am deeply convinced that, beyond all that he speaks of, there is much which he is silent about, even in his diary—

D

he is silent, and, probably, will never tell it to anyone. That " something " only occasionally and in
hints slipped through into his conversation, and hints
of it are also to be found in the two note-books of
his diary which he gave me and L. A. Sulerzhitsky
to read; it seems to me a kind of " negation of all
affirmations," the deepest and most evil nihilism
which has sprung from the soil of an infinite and
unrelieved despair, from a loneliness which, probably,
no one but he has experienced with such terrifying
clearness. I often thought him to be a man who in
the depths of his soul is stubbornly indifferent to
people: he is so much above and beyond them that
they seem to him like midges and their activities
ridiculous and miserable. He has gone too far away
from them into some desert, and there solitary, with
the highest effort of all the force of his spirit, he
closely examines into " the most essential," into
death.

All his life he feared and hated death, all his life
there throbbed in his soul the " Arsamasian terror "
—must he die ? The whole world, all the earth, looks
toward him; from China, India, America, from
everywhere, living, throbbing threads stretch out to
him; his soul is for all and for ever. Why should not
Nature make an exception to her law, give to one
man physical immortality—why not ? He is certainly

too rational and sensible to believe in miracles, but, on the other hand, he is a bogatyr, an explorer, and, like a young recruit, wild and headstrong from fear and despair in face of the unknown barrack. I remember in Gaspra he read Leo Shestov's book *Good and Evil in the Teaching of Nietzsche and Tolstoy*, and, when Anton Chekhov remarked that he did not like the book, Tolstoy said: " I thought it amusing. It's written swaggeringly, but it's all right and interesting. I'm sure I like cynics when they are sincere. Now he says: ' Truth is not wanted '; quite true, what should he want truth for ? For he will die all the same."

And, evidently seeing that his words had not been understood, he added with a quick smile:

" If a man has learned to think, no matter what he may think about, he is always thinking of his own death. All philosophers were like that. And what truths can there be, if there is death ? "

He went on to say that truth is the same for all— love of God; but on this subject he spoke coldly and wearily. After lunch on the terrace, he took up the book again, and, finding the passage, " Tolstoy, Dostoevsky, Nietzsche could not live without an answer to their questions, and for them any answer was better than none," he laughed and said:

" What a daring coiffeur; he says straight that I

deceived myself, and that means that I deceived others too. That is the obvious conclusion. . . ."

" Why coiffeur ? " asked Suler.

" Well," he answered thoughtfully, " it just came into my mind—he is fashionable, chic, and I remembered the coiffeur from Moscow at a wedding of his peasant uncle in the village. He has the finest manners and he dances fashionably, and so he despises everyone."

I repeat this conversation, I think, almost literally; it is most memorable for me, and I even wrote it down, as I did many other things which struck me. Sulerzhitsky and I wrote down many things which Tolstoy said, but Suler lost his notes when he came to me at Arsamas: he was habitually careless, and, although he loved Leo Nikolaevich like a woman, he behaved towards him rather strangely, almost like a superior. I have also mislaid my notes somewhere, and cannot find them; someone in Russia must have got them. I watched Tolstoy very attentively, because I was looking for—I am still looking for, and will until my death—a man with an active and a living faith. And also because once Anton Chekhov, speaking of our lack of culture, complained:

" Goethe's words were all recorded, but Tolstoy's thoughts are being lost in the air. That, my dear

fellow, is intolerably Russian. After his death they
will bestir themselves, will begin to write reminiscences, and will lie."

But to return to Shestov. " ' It is impossible,' he
says, ' to live looking at horrible ghosts,' but how
does *he* know whether it's horrible or not ? If he
knew, if he saw ghosts, he would not write this nonsense, but would do something serious, what Buddha
did all his life."

Someone remarked that Shestov was a Jew.

" Hardly," said Leo Nikolaevich doubtfully.

" No, he is not like a Jew; there are no disbelieving
Jews, you can't name one . . . no."

It seemed sometimes as though this old sorcerer
were playing with Death, coquetting with her, trying
somehow to deceive her, saying: " I am not afraid
of thee, I love thee, I long for thee."

And at the same time peering at Death with his
keen little eyes: " What art thou like ? What follows
thee hereafter ? Wilt thou destroy me altogether, or
will something in me go on living ? "

A strange impression used to be produced by his
words: " I am happy, I am awfully happy, I am too
happy." And then immediately afterwards: " To
suffer." To suffer—that, too, was true in him; I
don't doubt for a second that he, only half convales-
cent, would have been really glad to be put into

prison, to be banished—in a word, to embrace a martyr's crown. Would not martyrdom probably in some measure justify death, make her more understandable, acceptable from the external, from the formal point of view? But he was never happy, never and nowhere; I am certain of that: neither " in the books of wisdom," nor " on the back of a horse," nor " in the arms of a woman " did he experience the full delights of " earthly paradise." He is too rational for that and knows life and people too well. Here are some more of his words:

" The Kaliph Abdurahman had during his life fourteen happy days, but I am sure I have not had so many. And this is because I have never lived—I cannot live—for myself, for my own self; I live for show, for people."

When we left, Anton Chekhov said to me: " I don't believe that he was not happy." But I believe it. He was not. Though it is not true that he lived for show. Yes, what he himself did not need, he gave to people as though they were beggars; he liked to compel them, to compel them to read, walk, be vegetarians, love the peasants, and believe in the infallibility of the rational-religious reflections of Leo Tolstoy. People must be given something which will either satisfy or amuse them, and then let them be off. Let them leave a man in peace, to his habitual, tormenting, and sometimes cosy loneliness in face of the bottomless pit of the problem of " the essential."

All Russian preachers, with the exception of Avvakum and, perhaps, Tikhon Zadonsky, are cold men, for they did not possess an active and living faith. When I was writing Luka in *The Lower Depths*, I wanted to describe an old man like that: he is interested in " every solution," but not in people; coming inevitably in contact with them, he consoles them, but only in order that they may leave him in peace. And all the philosophy, all the preaching of such men, is alms bestowed by them with a veiled aversion, and there sounds behind their preaching words, which are beggarly and melancholy: " Get out! Love God or your neighbour, but get out! Curse God, love the stranger, but leave me alone! Leave me alone, for I am a man and I am doomed to death."

Alas, so it is and so it will be. It could not and cannot be otherwise, for men have become worn out, exhausted, terribly separated, and they are all chained to a loneliness which dries up the soul. If Leo Nikolaevich had had a reconciliation with the Church, it would not have at all surprised me. The thing would have had a logic of its own; all men are equally insignificant, even Archbishops. In fact, it would not have been a reconciliation, strictly speaking; for him personally the act would have been only logical: " I forgive those who hate me." It would have been a Christian act, and behind it there would have hidden a quick, ironical, little smile, which would be understood as the way in which a wise man retaliates on the fools.

What I write is not what I want to say; I cannot express it properly. There is a dog howling in my soul and I have a foreboding of some misfortune. Yes, newspapers have just arrived and it is already clear: you at home are beginning to " create a legend ": idlers and good-for-nothings have gone on living and have now produced a saint. Only think how pernicious it is for the country just at this moment, when the heads of disillusioned men are bowed down, the souls of the majority empty, and the souls of the best full of sorrow. Lacerated and starving, they long for a legend. They long so much for alleviation of pain, for the soothing of torment. And they will create just what he desires, but what is not wanted— the life of a holy man and saint; but surely he is great and holy because he is a man, a madly and tormentingly beautiful man; a man of the whole of mankind. I am somehow contradicting myself in this, but it does not matter. He is a man seeking God, not for himself, but for men, so that God may leave him, the man, alone in the peace of the desert chosen by him. He gave us the Gospels in order that we might forget the contradictions in Christ; he simplified Christ's image, smoothing away the militant elements and bringing into the foreground the humble " will of Him that sent Him." No doubt Tolstoy's Gospel is the more easily accepted because it is "soothing to the malady" of the Russian people. He had to give them something, for they complain and trouble the earth with their groaning and distract him from " the essential." But *War and Peace* and all the other things of the same kind will not soothe the sorrow and despair of the grey Russian land. Of *War and Peace* he himself said: " Without false modesty, it is like the *Iliad*." M. Y. Chaikovski heard from his lips exactly the same appreciation of *Childhood, Boyhood and Youth*.

Journalists have just arrived from Naples; one even hurried from Rome. They asked me to say what I think of Tolstoy's " flight "—" flight " is the word they use. I would not talk to them. You, of course, understand that inwardly I am terribly disturbed: I do not want to see Tolstoy a saint: let him remain a sinner close to the heart of the all-sinful world, even close to the heart of each one of us. Pushkin and he —there is nothing more sublime or dearer to us.

Leo Tolstoy is dead.

A telegram came containing the commonest of words—is dead.

It struck me to the heart: I cried with pain and anger, and now, half crazy, I imagine him as I know and saw him—I am tormented by a desire to speak with him. I imagine him in his coffin—he lies like a smooth stone at the bottom of a stream, and in his grey beard, I am sure, is quietly hidden that aloof, mysterious, little smile. And at last his hands are folded peacefully—they have finished their hard task.

I remember his keen eyes—they saw everything through and through—and the movements of his fingers, as though they were perpetually modelling something out of the air, his talk, his jokes, his favourite peasant words, his elusive voice. And I see what a vast amount of life was embodied in the man, how inhumanly clever he was, how terrifying.

I once saw him as, perhaps, no one has ever seen him. I was walking over to him at Gaspra along the coast, and behind Yusopov's estate, on the shore among the stones, I saw his smallish, angular figure in a grey, crumpled, ragged suit and crumpled hat. He was sitting with his head on his hands, the wind blowing the silvery hairs of his beard through his fingers: he was looking into the distance out to sea, and the little greenish waves rolled up obediently to

his feet and fondled them as though they were telling
something about themselves to the old magician. It
was a day of sun and cloud, and the shadows of the
clouds glided over the stones, and with the stones
the old man grew now bright and now dark. The
boulders were large, riven by cracks, and covered
with smelling seaweed: there had been a high tide.
He, too, seemed to me like an old stone come to life,
who knows all the beginnings and the ends of things,
who considers when and what will be the end of the
stones, the grasses of the earth, of the waters of the sea,
and of the whole universe from the pebble to the
sun. And the sea is part of his soul, and everything
around him comes from him, out of him. In the
musing motionlessness of the old man I felt something
fateful, magical, something which went down into
the darkness beneath him and stretched up, like a
searchlight, into the blue emptiness above the earth
—as though it were he, his concentrated will, which
was drawing the waves to him and repelling them,
which was ruling the movements of cloud and shadow,
which was stirring the stones to life. Suddenly, in a
moment of madness, I felt it is possible, he will get up,
wave his hand, and the sea will become solid and
glassy, the stones will begin to move and cry out,
everything around him will come to life, acquire a
voice, and speak in their different voices of themselves,

of him, against him. I cannot express in words what I felt rather than thought at that moment; in my soul there was joy and fear, and then everything blended in one happy thought: " I am not an orphan on the earth so long as this man lives on it."

Then I walked on tiptoe away in order that the pebbles might not scrunch under my feet, not wishing to distract his thoughts. And now I feel I am an orphan, I cry as I write—never before have I cried so unconsolably and in such bitter despair. I do not know whether I loved him; but does it matter, love of him or hatred ? He always roused in me sensations and agitations which were enormous, fantastic; even the unpleasant and hostile feelings which he aroused were of a kind not to oppress, but rather to explode the soul: they made it more sensitive and capacious. He was grand when, with his boots scraping over the ground, as though he were imperiously smoothing its unevenness, he suddenly appeared from somewhere, from behind a door or out of some corner, and came towards you with the short, light, quick step of a man accustomed to walk a great deal on the earth. With his thumbs in his belt he would stop for a second, looking round quickly with a comprehensive glance, a glance which at once took in anything new and instantly absorbed the meaning of everything.

" How do you do ? "

I always translated these words into: " How do you do ? There's pleasure for me, and for you there's not much sense in it—but still, how do you do ? "

He would come out looking rather small, and immediately everyone round him would become smaller than he. A peasant's beard, rough but extraordinary hands, simple clothes, all this external, comfortable democratism deceived many people, and I often saw how Russians who judge people by their clothes—an old slavish habit—began to pour out a stream of their odious " frankness," which is more properly called " the familiarity of the pigsty."

" Ah, you are one of us! That's what you are. At last, by God's grace, I am face to face with the greatest son of our native land. Hail for ever. I bow low to you."

That is a sample of Muscovite Russian, simple and hearty, and here is another, but " free-thinkerish ":

" Leo Nikolaevich, though I disagree with your religious-philosophical views, I deeply respect in your person the greatest of artists."

And suddenly, under his peasant's beard, under his democratic crumpled blouse, there would rise the old Russian *barin*, the grand aristocrat: then the noses of the simple-hearted visitor, educated and all the rest, instantly became blue with intolerable cold. It was pleasant to see this creature of the purest blood, to watch the noble grace of his gestures, the proud reserve of his speech, to hear the exquisite pointedness of his murderous words. He showed just as much of the *barin* as was needed for these serfs, and when they called out the *barin* in Tolstoy it appeared naturally and easily and crushed them so that they shrivelled up and whined.

One day I was returning from Yasnaya Polyana to Moscow with one of these " simple-hearted " Russians, a Moscow man, and for a long time he could not recover his breath, but kept on smiling woefully and repeating in astonishment: " Well, well, that was a cold bath. He's severe . . . pooh! "

And in the middle of it all he exclaimed, apparently with regret: " And I thought he was really an anarchist. Everyone keeps on saying: ' Anarchist, anarchist,' and I believed it. . . ."

The man was a large, rich manufacturer, with a great belly, and a face the colour of raw meat—why did he want Tolstoy to be an anarchist ? One of the " profound mysteries " of the Russian soul!

When Leo Nikolaevich wished to please, he could do so more easily than a clever and beautiful woman. Imagine a company of people of all kinds sitting in his room: the Grand Duke Nicolai Mikhailovich, the house-painter Ilya, a social-democrat from Yalta, the stundist Patzuk, a musician, a German, the manager of the estates of Countess Kleinmichel, the poet Bulgakov, and all look at him with the same enamoured eyes. He explains to them the teaching of Lao-Tse, and he seems to me an extraordinary man-orchestra, possessing the faculty of playing several instruments at the same time, a brass trumpet, a drum, harmonium, and flute. I used to look at him just as the others did. And now I long to see him once more—and I shall never see him again.

Journalists have come asserting that a telegram has been received in Rome " denying the rumour of Tolstoy's death." They bustled and chattered, redundantly expressing their sympathy with Russia. The Russian newspapers leave no room for doubt.

To lie to him, even out of pity, was impossible; even when he was seriously ill, one could not pity him. It would be banal to pity a man like him. They ought to be taken care of, cherished, not loaded with the wordy dust of worn-out, soulless words.

He used to ask: " You don't like me ? " and one had to answer: " No, I don't."

" You don't love me ? "—" No, to-day I don't love you."

In his questions he was merciless, in his answers reserved, as becomes a wise man.

He used to speak with amazing beauty of the past, and particularly of Turgenev; of Fet always with a good-natured smile and always something amusing, of Nekrasov coldly and sceptically; but of all writers exactly as if they were his children and he, the father, knew all their faults, and—there you are!

He would point out their faults before their merits, and every time he blamed someone it seemed to me that he was giving alms to his listeners because of their poverty; to listen to him then made one feel awkward, one's eyes fell before his sharp little smile and—nothing remained in one's memory.

Once he argued fiercely that G. Y. Uspensky wrote in the Tula dialect, and had no talent at all. And later I heard him say to Anton Pavlovich Chekhov: "He (Uspensky) is a writer! In the power of his sincerity he recalls Dostoevsky, only Dostoevsky went in for politics and coquetted, while Uspensky is more simple and sincere. If he had believed in God, he would have been a sectarian."

"But you said he was a Tula writer and had no talent."

He drew his shaggy brows down over his eyes and said: "He wrote badly. What kind of language does he use? There are more punctuation marks than words. Talent is love. One who loves is talented. Look at lovers, they are all talented."

Of Dostoevsky he spoke reluctantly, constrainedly, evading or repressing something: "He ought to have

made himself acquainted with the teaching of Con-
fucius or the Buddhists; that would have calmed him
down. That is the chief thing which everyone should
know. He was a man of rebellious flesh; when angry,
bumps would suddenly rise on his bald head; and his
ears would move. He felt a great deal, but he thought
poorly; it is from the Fourierists, from Butashevich
and the others, that he learnt to think. And afterwards all his life long he hated them. There was
something Jewish in his blood. He was suspicious
without reason, ambitious, heavy and unfortunate.
It is curious that he is so much read. I can't understand why. It is all painful and useless, because all
those Idiots, Adolescents, Raskolnikovs, and the rest
of them, they are not real; it is all much simpler,
more understandable. It's a pity people don't read
Lyeskov, he's a real writer—have you read him ? "

" Yes, I like him very much, especially his language."

" He knew the language marvellously, even the
tricks. Strange that you should like him; somehow
you are not Russian, your thoughts are not Russian
—is it all right, you're not hurt at my saying that ?
I am an old man, and, perhaps, I can no longer
understand modern literature, but it seems to me
that it is all not Russian. They began to write a
curious kind of verse; I don't know what these poems

E

are or what they mean. One has to learn to write poetry from Pushkin, Tyuchev, Fet. Now you "—he turned to Chekhov—" you are Russian. Yes, very, very Russian."

And smiling affectionately, he put his hand on Chekhov's shoulder; and the latter became uncomfortable and began in a low voice to mutter something about his bungalow and the Tartars.

He loved Chekhov, and, when he looked at him, his eyes were tender and seemed almost to stroke Anton Pavlovich's face. Once, when Anton Pavlovich was walking on the lawn with Alexandra Lvovna, Tolstoy, who at the time was still ill and was sitting in a chair on the terrace, seemed to stretch towards them, saying in a whisper: " Ah, what a beautiful, magnificent man: modest and quiet like a girl! And he walks like a girl. He's simply wonderful."

One evening, in the twilight, half closing his eyes and moving his brows, he read a variant of the scene in *Father Sergius*, where the woman goes to seduce the hermit: he read it through to the end, and then, raising his head and shutting his eyes, he said distinctly: " The old man wrote it well, well."

It came out with such amazing simplicity, his pleasure in its beauty was so sincere, that I shall never forget the delight which it gave me at the time, a delight which I could not—did not know how to express, but which I could only suppress by a tremendous effort. My heart stopped beating for a moment, and then everything around me seemed to become fresh and revivified.

One must have heard him speak in order to understand the extraordinary, indefinable beauty of his speech; it was, in a sense, incorrect, abounding in repetitions of the same word, saturated with village simplicity. The effect of his words did not come only from the intonation and the expression of his face, but from the play and light in his eyes, the most eloquent eyes I have ever seen. In his two eyes Leo Nikolaevich possessed a thousand eyes.

Once Suler, Sergei Lvovich, Chekhov, and someone else, were sitting in the park and talking about women; he listened in silence for a long time, and then suddenly said:

" And I will tell the truth about women, when I have one foot in the grave—I shall tell it, jump into my coffin, pull the lid over me, and say, ' Do what you like now.' " The look he gave us was so wild, so terrifying, that we all fell silent for a while.

He had in him, I think, the inquisitive, mischievous wildness of a Vaska Buslaév, and also something of the stubbornness of soul of the Protopope Avvakum, while above or at his side lay hidden the scepticism

of a Chaadaev. The Avvakumian element harried
and tormented with its preachings the artist in him;
the Novgorod wildness upset Shakespeare and Dante,
while the Chaadaevian element scoffed at his soul's
amusements and, by the way, at its agonies. And the
old Russian man in him dealt a blow at science and
the State, the Russian driven to the passivity of
anarchism by the barrenness of all his efforts to build
up a more human life.

Strange! This Buslaev characteristic in Tolstoy was
perceived through some mysterious intuition by Olaf
Gulbranson, the caricaturist of *Simplicissimus*: look
closely at his drawing and you will see how startlingly
he has got the likeness of the real Tolstoy, what
intellectual daring there is in that face with its veiled
and hidden eyes, for which nothing is sacred and
which believe " neither in a sneeze, nor a dream, nor
the cawing of a bird."

The old magician stands before me, alien to all, a
solitary traveller through all the deserts of thought in
search of an all-embracing truth which he has not
found—I look at him and, although I feel sorrow for
the loss, I feel pride at having seen the man, and that
pride alleviates my pain and grief.

It was curious to see Leo Nikolaevich among
" Tolstoyans "; there stands a noble belfry and its
bell sounds untiringly over the whole world, while

round about run tiny, timorous dogs whining at the
bell and distrustfully looking askance at one another
as though to say, " Who howled best ? " I always
thought that these people infected the Yasnaya
Polyana house, as well as the great house of Countess
Panin, with a spirit of hypocrisy, cowardice, mer-
cenary and self-seeking pettiness and legacy-hunting.
The " Tolstoyans " have something in common with
those friars who wander in all the dark corners of
Russia, carrying with them dogs' bones and passing
them off as relics, selling " Egyptian darkness " and
the " little tears of Our Lady." One of these apostles,
I remember, at Yasnaya Polyana refused to eat eggs
so as not to wrong the hens, but at Tula railway-
station he greedily devoured meat, saying: " The
old fellow does exaggerate."

Nearly all of them like to moan and kiss one
another; they all have boneless perspiring hands and
lying eyes. At the same time they are practical
fellows and manage their earthly affairs cleverly.

Leo Nikolaevich, of course, well understood the
value of the " Tolstoyans," and so did Sulerzhitsky,
whom Tolstoy loved tenderly and whom he always
spoke of with a kind of youthful ardour and fervour.
Once one of those " Tolstoyans " at Yasnaya Polyana
explained eloquently how happy his life had become
and how pure his soul after he accepted Tolstoy's

teaching. Leo Nikolaevich leant over and said to me in a low voice: " He's lying all the time, the rogue, but he does it to please me. . . ."

Many tried to please him, but I did not observe that they did it well or with any skill. He rarely spoke to me on his usual subjects of universal forgiveness, loving one's neighbour, the Gospels, and Buddhism, evidently because he realized at once that all that would not " go down " with me. I greatly appreciated this.

When he liked he could be extraordinarily charming, sensitive, and tactful; his talk was fascinatingly simple and elegant, but sometimes it was painfully unpleasant to listen to him. I always disliked what he said about women—it was unspeakably " vulgar," and there was in his words something artificial, insincere, and at the same time very personal. It seemed as if he had once been hurt, and could neither forget nor forgive. The evening when I first got to know him, he took me into his study—it was at Khamovniki in Moscow—and, making me sit opposite to him, began to talk about *Varenka Oliessova* and of *Twenty-Six and One*. I was overwhelmed by his tone and lost my head, he spoke so plainly and brutally, arguing that in a healthy girl chastity is not natural. " If a girl who has turned fifteen is healthy, she desires to be touched and embraced. Her mind is still afraid of the unknown and of what she does not understand—that is what they call chastity and purity. But her flesh is already aware that the incomprehensible is right, lawful, and, in spite of the mind, it demands fulfilment of the law. Now you describe Varenka Oliessova as healthy, but her feelings are anæmic—that is not true to life."

Then he began to speak about the girl in *Twenty-Six and One*, using a stream of indecent words with a simplicity which seemed to me cynical and even offended me. Later I came to see that he used unmentionable words only because he found them more precise and pointed, but at the time it was unpleasant to me to listen to him. I made no reply, and suddenly he became attentive and kindly and began asking me about my life, what I was studying, and what I read.

" I am told that you are very well read; is that true ? Is Korelenko a musician ? "

" I believe not; but I'm not sure."

" You don't know ? Do you like his stories ? "

" I do very much."

" It is the contrast. He is lyrical and you haven't got that. Have you read Weltmann ? "

" Yes."

" Isn't he a good writer, clever, exact, and with no

exaggeration? He is sometimes better than Gogol.
He knew Balzac. And Gogol imitated Marlinski."

When I said that Gogol was probably influenced
by Hoffmann, Sterne, and perhaps Dickens, he
glanced at me and asked: " Have you read that
somewhere? No? It isn't true. Gogol hardly
knew Dickens. But you must clearly have read a
great deal: now look here, it's dangerous. Kolzov
ruined himself by it."

When he accompanied me to the door, he embraced
and kissed me and said: " You are a real mouzhik.
You will find it difficult to live among writers, but
never mind, don't be afraid, always say what you feel,
even if it be rude—it doesn't matter. Sensible people
will understand."

I had two impressions from this first meeting: I was
glad and proud to have seen Tolstoy, but his conversation reminded me a little of an examination,
and in a sense I did not see in him the author of
Cossacks, *Kholstomier*, *War and Peace*, but a *barin* who,
making allowances for me, considered it necessary to
speak to me in the common language, the language of
the street and market-place. That upset my idea of
him, an idea which was deeply rooted and had become
dear to me.

It was at Yasnaya Polyana that I saw him again.
It was an overcast, autumn day with a drizzle of rain,

and he put on a heavy overcoat and high leather
boots and took me for a walk in the birch wood. He
jumped the ditches and pools like a boy, shook the
raindrops off the branches, and gave me a superb
account of how Fet had explained Schopenhauer to
him in this wood. He stroked the damp, satin trunks
of the birches lovingly with his hand and said:
" Lately I read a poem:

> The mushrooms are gone, but in the hollows
> Is the heavy smell of mushroom dampness. . . .

Very good, very true."

Suddenly a hare got up under our feet. Leo
Nikolaevich started up excited, his face lit up, and
he whooped like a real old sportsman. Then, looking
at me with a curious little smile, he broke into a
sensible, human laugh. He was wonderfully charming at that moment.

Another time he was looking at a hawk in the park:
it was hovering over the cattle-shed, making wide
circles suspended in the air, moving its wings very
slightly as if undecided whether or not the moment
to strike had come. Leo Nikolaevich stood up shading
his eyes with his hand and murmured with excitement: " The rogue is going for our chickens. Now,
now . . . it's coming . . . O, he's afraid. The
groom is there, isn't he ? I'll call the groom. . . ."

And he shouted to the groom. When he shouted,

the hawk was scared, swept upwards, swung away
and disappeared. Leo Nikolaevich sighed, apparently
reproaching himself, and said: " I should not have
shouted; he would have struck all the same. . . ."

Once in telling him about Tiflis, I mentioned the
name of V. V. Flerovsky-Bervi. " Did you know
him ? " Leo Nikolaevich asked with interest: " Tell
me, what is he like ? "

I told him about Flerovsky: tall, long-bearded,
thin, with very large eyes; how he used to wear a
long, sail-cloth blouse, and how, armed with a bundle
of rice, cooked in red wine, tied in his belt, and an
enormous linen umbrella, he wandered with me on
the mountain paths of Trans-Caucasia; how once
on a narrow path we met a buffalo and prudently
retreated, threatening the brute with the open
umbrella, and, every time we stepped back, in danger
of falling over the precipice. Suddenly I noticed that
there were tears in Tolstoy's eyes, and this confused
me and I stopped.

" Never mind," he said, " go on, go on. It's pleasure at hearing about a good man. I imagined him just
like that, unique. Of all the radicals he is the most
mature and clever; in his *Alphabet* he proves con-
clusively that all our civilization is barbarian, that
culture is the work of the peaceful and weak, not the
strong, nations, and that the struggle for existence is a

lying invention by which it is sought to justify evil. You, of course, don't agree with this ? But Daudet agrees, you know, you remember his Paul Astier ? "

" But how would you reconcile Flerovsky's theory, say, with the part played by the Normans in the history of Europe ? "

" The Normans ? That's another thing."

If he did not want to answer, he would always say: " That's another thing."

It always seemed to me—and I do not think I was mistaken—that Leo Nikolaevich was not very fond of talking about literature, but was vitally interested in the personality of an author. The questions: " Do you know him ? What is he like ? Where was he born ? " I often heard in his mouth. And nearly all his opinions would throw some curious light upon a man.

Of V. K. he said thoughtfully: " He is not a Great Russian, and so he must see our life better and more truly than we do." Of Anton Chekhov, whom he loved dearly: " His medicine gets in his way; if he were not a doctor, he would be a still better writer." Of one of the younger writers: " He pretends to be an Englishman, and in that character a Moscow man has the least success." To me he once said: " You are an inventor: all these Kuvaldas of yours are inventions." When I answered that Kuvalda had

been drawn from life, he said: " Tell me, where did
you see him ? "

He laughed heartily at the scene in the court of the
Kazan magistrate, Konovalov, where I had first seen
the man whom I described under the name of
Kuvalda. " Blue blood," he said, wiping the tears
from his eyes, " that's it—blue blood. But how
splendid, how amusing. You tell it better than you
write it. Yes, you are an inventor, a romantic, you
must confess."

I said that probably all writers are to some extent
inventors, describing people as they would like to see
them in life; I also said that I liked active people who
desire to resist the evil of life by every means, even
violence.

" And violence is the chief evil," he exclaimed,
taking me by the arm. " How will you get out of
that contradiction, inventor ? Now your *My Travelling
Companion* isn't invented—it's good just because it
isn't invented. But when you think, you beget
knights, all Amadises and Siegfrieds."

I remarked that as long as we live in the narrow
sphere of our anthropomorphous and unavoidable
" travelling companions," we build everything on
quicksands and in a hostile medium.

He smiled and nudged me slightly with his elbow:
" From that very, very dangerous conclusions can be

drawn. You are a questionable Socialist. You are a romantic, and romantics must be monarchists—they always have been."

" And Hugo ? "

" Hugo ? That's another thing I don't like him, a noisy man."

He often asked me what I was reading, and always reproached me if I had chosen, in his opinion, a bad book.

" Gibbon is worse than Kostomarov; one ought to read Mommsen, he's very tedious, but it's all so solid."

When he heard that the first book I ever read was *The Brothers Semganno*, he even got angry: " Now, you see—a stupid novel. That's what has spoilt you. The French have three writers, Stendhal, Balzac, Flaubert; and, well, perhaps Maupassant, though Chekhov is better than he. The Goncourts are mere clowns, they only pretended to be serious. They had studied life from books written by inventors like themselves, and they thought it a serious business; but it was of no use to a soul."

I disagreed with this opinion, and it irritated Leo Nikolaevich a little; he could barely stand contradiction, and sometimes his opinions were strange and capricious.

" There is no such thing as degeneration," he said

once. " The Italian Lombroso invented it, and after him comes the Jew Nordau, screaming like a parrot. Italy is the land of charlatans and adventurers: only Aretinos, Casanovas, Cagliostros, and the like are born there."

" And Garibaldi ? "

" That's politics; that's another thing."

To a whole series of facts, taken from the life of the merchant-class families in Russia, he answered: " But it's untrue; it's only written in clever books."

I told him the actual history of three generations of a merchant family which I had known, a history in which the law of degeneration had acted with particular mercilessness. Then he began excitedly tugging at my arm and encouraging me to write about it: " Now that's true. I know it; there are two families like that in Tula. It ought to be written. A long novel, written concisely, do you see ? You must do it." His eyes flashed.

" But then there will be knights, Leo Nikolaevich."

" Don't. This is really serious. The one who is going to be a monk and pray for the whole family —it's wonderful. That's real: you sin and I will go and expiate your sin by prayer. And the other, the weary one, the money-loving founder of the family— that's true, too. And he's a drunken, profligate beast, and loves everyone, and suddenly commits murder

—ah, it's good. It should be written, among thieves and beggars you must not look for heroes, you really mustn't. Heroes—that's a lie and invention; there are simply people, people, and nothing else."

He often pointed out exaggerations in my stories, but once, speaking of *Dead Souls*, he said, smiling good-naturedly:

" We are all of us terrible inventors. I myself, when I write, suddenly feel pity for some character, and then I give him some good quality or take a good quality away from someone else, so that in comparison with the others he may not appear too black." And then in the stern tones of an inexorable judge: " That's why I say that art is a lie, an arbitrary sham, harmful for people. One writes not what real life is, but simply what one thinks of life oneself. What good is that to anyone, how I see that tower or sea or Tartar—what interest or use is there in it ? " Once I was walking with him on the lower road from Dyulbev to Ai-Todor On; he was walking with the light step of a young man, when he said to me more nervously than was usual with him: " The flesh should be the obedient dog of the spirit, running to do its bidding; but we—how do we live ? The flesh rages and riots, and the spirit follows it helpless and miserable."

He rubbed his chest hard over the heart, raised his

eyebrows, and then, remembering something, went on: " One autumn in Moscow in an alley near the Sukharev Gate I once saw a drunken woman lying in the gutter. A stream of filthy water flowed from the yard of a house right under her neck and back. She lay in that cold liquid, muttering, shivering, wriggling her body in the wet, but she could not get up."

He shuddered, half closed his eyes, shook his head, and went on gently: " Let's sit down here. . . . It's the most horrible and disgusting thing, a drunken woman. I wanted to help her get up, but I couldn't; I felt such a loathing; she was so slippery and slimy— I felt that if I'd touched her, I could not have washed my hand clean for a month—horrible. And on the kerb sat a bright, grey-eyed boy, the tears running down his cheeks: he was sobbing and repeating wearily and helplessly: ' Mu-um . . . mu-um-my . . . do get up.' She would move her arms, grunt, lift her head, and again—bang went her neck into the filth."

He was silent, and then looking round, he repeated almost in a whisper: " Yes, yes, horrible. You've seen many drunken women ? Many—my God! You, you must not write about that, you mustn't."

" Why ? "

He looked straight into my eyes and, smiling, repeated: " Why ? " Then thoughtfully and slowly he said: " I don't know. It just slipped out . . . it's a shame to write about filth. But yet why not write about it ? Yes, it's necessary to write all about everything, everything."

Tears came into his eyes. He wiped them away, and, smiling, he looked at his handkerchief, while the tears again ran down his wrinkles. " I am crying," he said. " I am an old man. It cuts me to the heart when I remember something horrible."

And very gently touching me with his elbow, he said: " You, too—you will have lived your life, and everything will remain exactly as it was, and then you, too, will cry worse than I, more ' streamingly,' as the peasant women say. And everything must be written about, everything; otherwise that bright little boy might be hurt, he might reproach us—' it's untrue, it's not the whole truth,' he will say. He's strict for the truth."

Suddenly he gave himself a shake and said in a kind voice: " Now, tell me a story; you tell them well. Something about a child, about your childhood. It's not easy to believe that you were once a child. You are a strange creature, exactly as if you were born grown-up. In your ideas there is a good deal of the childlike and the immature, but you know more than enough of life—and one cannot ask for more. Well, tell me a story. . . ."

F

He lay down comfortably upon the bare roots of a pine tree and watched the ants moving busily among the grey spines.

In the South, which, with its self-asserting luxuriance and flaunting, unbridled vegetation, seems so strangely incongruous to a man from the North, he, Leo Tolstoy—even his name speaks of his inner power —seemed a small man, but knitted and knotted out of very strong roots deep in the earth—in the flaunting scenery of the Crimea, I say, he was at once both out of place and in his place. He seemed a very ancient man, master of all his surroundings—a master builder who, after centuries of absence, has arrived in the mansion built by him. He has forgotten a great deal which it contains; much is new to him; everything is as it should be, and yet not entirely so, and he has at once to find out what is amiss and why it is amiss.

He walked the roads and paths with a business-like, quick step of the skilled explorer of the earth, and with sharp eyes, from which neither a single pebble nor a single thought could hide itself, he looked, measured, tested, compared. And he scattered about him the living seeds of indomitable thoughts. He said to Suler once: " You, Liovushka, read nothing which is not good out of self-conceit, while Gorky reads a lot which is not good, because he distrusts himself. I write much which is not good, because of an old man's ambition, a desire that all should think as I do. Of course, I think it is good, and Gorky thinks it is not good, and you think nothing at all; you simply blink and watch what you may clutch. One day you will clutch something which does not belong to you—it has happened to you before. You will put your claws into it, hold on for a bit, and when it begins to get loose, you won't try to stop it. Chekhov has a superb story, *The Darling*—you are rather like her."

" In what ? " asked Suler, laughing.

" You can love well, but to choose—no, you can't, and you will waste yourself on trifles."

" Is everyone like that ? "

" Everyone ? " Leo Nikolaevich repeated. " No, not everyone."

And suddenly he asked me, exactly as if he were dealing me a blow: " Why don't you believe in God ? "

" I have no faith, Leo Nikolaevich."

" It is not true. By nature you are a believer, and you cannot get on without God. You will realize it one day. Your disbelief comes from obstinacy, because you have been hurt: the world is not what you would like it to be. There are also some people who do not believe out of shyness; it happens with young people; they adore some woman, but don't want to show it from fear that she won't understand, and also from lack of courage. Faith, like love, requires courage and daring. One has to say to one-self ' I believe,' and everything will come right, everything will appear as you want it, it will explain itself to you and attract you. Now, you love much, and faith is only a greater love: you must love still more, and then your love will turn to faith. When one loves a woman, she is, unfailingly, the best woman on earth, and each loves the best woman, and that is faith. A non-believer cannot love: to-day he falls in love with one woman, and next year with another. The souls of such men are tramps living barren lives—that is not good. But you were born a believer, and it is no use thwarting yourself. Well, you may say beauty? And what is beauty? The highest and most perfect is God."

He hardly ever spoke to me on this subject, and its seriousness and the suddenness of it rather over-whelmed me. I was silent.

He was sitting on the couch with his legs drawn up under him, and breaking into a triumphant little smile and shaking his finger at me, he said: " You won't get out of this by silence, no."

And I, who do not believe in God, looked at him for some reason very cautiously and a little timidly, I looked and thought: " The man is godlike."

ANTON CHEKHOV:
FRAGMENTS OF RECOLLECTIONS

Translated from the Russian by
S. S. KOTELIANSKY AND
LEONARD WOOLF

These reminiscences of Chekhov by Gorky
appeared in Russia in 1906. This is the
only translation into English that has been
published

ANTON CHEKHOV:
FRAGMENTS OF RECOLLECTIONS

ONCE he invited me to the village Kutchuk-Koy, where he had a tiny strip of land, and a white, two-storied house. There, while showing me his " estate," he began to speak with animation: " If I had plenty of money, I should build a sanatorium here for invalid village teachers. You know, I would put up a large, bright building—very bright, with large windows and lofty rooms. I would have a fine library, different musical instruments, bees, a vegetable garden, an orchard. . . . There would be lectures on agriculture, meteorology. . . . Teachers ought to know everything—everything, my dear fellow."

He was suddenly silent, coughed, looked at me out of the corner of his eyes, and smiled that tender, charming smile of his which attracted one so irresistibly to him and made one listen so attentively to his words.

" Does it bore you to listen to my fantasies ? I do love to talk of it. . . . If you knew how badly the Russian village needs a nice, sensible, educated teacher! We ought in Russia to give the teacher particularly good conditions, and it ought to be done as quickly as possible. We ought to realize that without a wide education of the people, Russia will collapse like a house built of badly baked bricks. A teacher must be an artist, in love with his calling; but with us he is a journeyman, ill-educated, who goes to the village to teach children as though he were going into exile. He is starved, crushed, terrorized by the fear of losing his daily bread. But he ought to be the first man in the village; the peasants ought to recognize him as a power, worthy of attention and respect; no one should dare to shout at him or humiliate him personally, as with us everyone does—the village constable, the rich shopkeeper, the priest, the rural police commissioner, the school guardian, the councillor, and that official who has won the title of school-inspector, but who cares nothing for the improvement of education and only sees that the circulars of his chiefs are carried out. . . . It is ridiculous to pay in farthings the man who has to educate the people. It is intolerable that he should walk in rags, shiver with cold in damp and draughty schools, catch cold, and about the age of thirty get laryngitis, rheumatism, or tuberculosis. We ought to be ashamed of it. Our teacher, for eight or nine months in the year, lives like a hermit: he has no one to speak a word to; without company, books, or amusements, he is growing stupid, and, if he invites his colleagues to visit him, then he becomes politically suspect—a stupid word with which crafty men frighten fools. All this is disgusting; it is the mockery of a man who is doing a great and tremendously important work. . . . Do you know, whenever I see a teacher, I feel ashamed for him, for his timidity, and because he is badly dressed . . . it seems to me that for the teacher's wretchedness I am myself to blame—I mean it."

He was silent, thinking; and then, waving his hand, he said gently: " This Russia of ours is such an absurd, clumsy country."

A shadow of sadness crossed his beautiful eyes: little rays of wrinkles surrounded them and made them look still more meditative. Then, looking round, he said jestingly: " You see, I have fired off at you a complete leading article from a Radical paper. Come, I'll give you tea to reward your patience."

That was characteristic of him, to speak so earnestly, with such warmth and sincerity and then suddenly to laugh at himself and his speech. In that sad and gentle smile one felt the subtle scepticism of the man who knows the value of words and dreams; and there also flashed in the smile a lovable modesty and delicate sensitiveness.

We walked back slowly in silence to the house. It

was a clear, hot day; the waves sparkled under the bright rays of the sun; down below one heard a dog barking joyfully. Chekhov took my arm, coughed, and said slowly: " It is shameful and sad, but true: there are many men who envy the dogs."

And he added immediately with a laugh: " To-day I can only make feeble speeches. . . . It means that I'm getting old."

I often heard him say: " You know, a teacher has just come here . . . he's ill, married . . . couldn't you do something for him? I have made arrangements for him for the time being." Or again: " Listen, Gorky, there is a teacher here who would like to meet you. He can't go out, he's ill. Won't you come and see him? Do." Or: " Look here, the women teachers want books to be sent to them."

Sometimes I would find that " teacher " at his house; usually he would be sitting on the edge of his chair, blushing at the consciousness of his own awkwardness, in the sweat of his brow picking and choosing his words, trying to speak smoothly and " educatedly," or, with the ease of manner of a person who is morbidly shy, he would concentrate himself upon the effort not to appear stupid in the eyes of an author, and he would simply belabour Anton Chekhov with a hail of questions which had never entered his head until that moment.

Anton Chekhov would listen attentively to the dreary, incoherent speech; now and again a smile came into his sad eyes, a little wrinkle appeared on his forehead, and then, in his soft, lustreless voice, he began to speak simple, clear, homely words, words which somehow or other immediately made his questioner simple: the teacher stopped trying to be clever, and therefore immediately became more clever and interesting. . . .

I remember one teacher, a tall, thin man with a yellow, hungry face, and a long, hooked nose which dropped gloomily towards his chin. He sat opposite Anton Chekhov and, looking fixedly into Chekhov's face with his black eyes, said in a melancholy bass voice:

" From such impressions of existence within the space of the tutorial session there comes a psychical conglomeration which crushes every possibility of an objective attitude towards the surrounding universe. Of course, the universe is nothing but our presentation of it. . . ."

And he rushed headlong into philosophy, and he moved over its surface like a drunkard skating on ice.

" Tell me," Chekhov put in quietly and kindly, " who is that teacher in your district who beats the children ? "

The teacher sprang from his chair and waved his

arms indignantly: " Whom do you mean ? Me ?
Never. Beating ? "

He snorted with indignation.

" Don't get excited," Anton Chekhov went on,
smiling reassuringly; " I'm not speaking of you.
But I remember—I read it in the newspapers—there
is someone in your district who beats the children."

The teacher sat down, wiped his perspiring face,
and, with a sigh of relief, said in his deep bass:

" It's true . . . there was such a case . . . it was
Makarov. You know, it's not surprising. It's cruel,
but explicable. He's married . . . has four children
. . . his wife is ill . . . himself consumptive . . .
his salary is twenty roubles, the school like a cellar,
and the teacher has but a single room—under such
circumstances you will give a thrashing to an angel of
God for no fault . . . and the children—they're far
from angels, believe me."

And the man who had just been mercilessly
belabouring Chekhov with his store of clever words,
suddenly, ominously wagging his hooked nose, began
to speak simple, weighty, clear-cut words, which
illuminated, like a fire, the terrible, accursed truth
about the life of the Russian village.

When he said good-bye to his host, the teacher
took Chekhov's small, dry hand with its thin fingers
in both his own, and, shaking it, said:

" I came to you as though I were going to the authorities, in fear and trembling . . . I puffed myself out like a turkey-cock . . . I wanted to show you that I was no ordinary mortal. . . . And now I'm leaving you as a nice, close friend who understands everything. It's a great thing—to understand everything! Thank you! I'm taking away with me a pleasant thought: big men are simpler and more understandable . . . and nearer in soul to us fellow men than all those wretches among whom we live. . . . Good-bye; I will never forget you."

His nose quivered, his lips twisted into a good-natured smile, and he added suddenly:

" To tell the truth, scoundrels, too, are unhappy—the devil take them."

When he went out, Chekhov followed him with a glance, smiled, and said:

" He's a nice fellow. . . . He won't be a teacher long."

" Why ? "

" They will run him down—whip him off."

He thought for a bit, and added quietly: " In Russia an honest man is rather like the chimney-sweep with whom nurses frighten children."

.   .   .   .   .   .

I think that in Anton Chekhov's presence everyone involuntarily felt in himself a desire to be simpler,

G

more truthful, more oneself; I often saw how people
cast off the motley finery of bookish phrases, smart
words, and all the other cheap tricks with which a
Russian, wishing to figure as a European, adorns
himself, like a savage with shells and fish's teeth.
Anton Chekhov disliked fish's teeth and cock's
feathers; anything " brilliant " or foreign, assumed
by a man to make himself look bigger, disturbed him;
I noticed that, whenever he saw anyone dressed up
in this way, he had a desire to free him from all that
oppressive, useless tinsel, and to find underneath the
genuine face and living soul of the person. All his life
Chekhov lived on his own soul; he was always himself, inwardly free, and he never troubled about what
some people expected and others—coarser people—
demanded of Anton Chekhov. He did not like conversations about deep questions, conversations with
which our dear Russians so assiduously comfort themselves, forgetting that it is ridiculous, and not at all
amusing, to argue about velvet costumes in the future
when in the present one has not even a decent pair of
trousers.

Beautifully simple himself, he loved everything
simple, genuine, sincere, and he had a peculiar way
of making other people simple.

Once, I remember, three luxuriously dressed ladies
came to see him; they filled his room with the rustle

of silk skirts and the smell of strong scent; they sat down politely opposite their host, pretended that they were interested in politics, and began " putting questions " :

" Anton Pavlovich, what do you think ? How will the war end ? "

Anton Pavlovich coughed, thought for a while, and then gently, in a serious and kindly voice, replied:

" Probably in peace."

" Well, yes . . . certainly. But who will win ? The Greeks or the Turks ? "

" It seems to me that those will win who are the stronger."

" And who, do you think, are the stronger ? " all the ladies asked together.

" Those who are the better fed and the better educated."

" Ah, how clever," one of them exclaimed.

" And whom do you like best ? " another asked.

Anton Pavlovich looked at her kindly, and answered with a meek smile:

" I love candied fruits . . . don't you ? "

" Very much," the lady exclaimed gaily.

" Especially Abrikossov's," the second agreed solidly.

And the third, half closing her eyes, added with relish:

" It smells so good."

And all three began to talk with vivacity, revealing on the subject of candied fruit great erudition and subtle knowledge. It was obvious that they were happy at not having to strain their minds and pretend to be seriously interested in Turks and Greeks, to whom up to that moment they had not given a thought.

When they left they merrily promised Anton Pavlovich:

" We will send you some candied fruit."

" You managed that nicely," I observed when they had gone.

Anton Pavlovich laughed quietly and said:

" Everyone should speak his own language."

On another occasion I found at his house a young and prettyish Crown Prosecutor. He was standing in front of Chekhov, shaking his curly head, and speaking briskly:

" In your story, *The Conspirator*, you, Anton Pavlovich, put before me a very complex case. If I admit in Denis Grigoryev an evil and conscious intention, then I must, without any reservation, bundle him into prison, in the interests of the community. But he is a savage: he did not realize the criminality of his act. . . . I feel pity for him. But suppose I regard him as a man who acted without understanding, and suppose I yield to my feeling of pity, how can I guarantee the community that Denis will not again unscrew the nut in the sleepers and wreck a train ? That's the question. What's to be done ? "

He stopped, threw himself back, and fixed an inquiring look on Anton Pavlovich's face. His uniform was quite new, and the buttons shone as self-confidently and dully on his chest as did the little eyes in the pretty, clean little face of the youthful enthusiast for justice.

" If I were judge," said Anton Pavlovich gravely, " I would acquit Denis."

" On what grounds ? "

" I would say to him, ' You, Denis, have not yet ripened into the type of the deliberate criminal; go —and ripen.' "

The lawyer began to laugh, but instantly again became pompously serious, and said:

" No, sir, the question put by you must be answered only in the interests of the community, whose life and property I am called upon to protect. Denis is a savage, but he is also a criminal—that is the truth."

" Do you like gramophones ? " suddenly asked Anton Pavlovich in his soft voice.

" Oh yes, very much. An amazing invention," the youth answered gaily.

" And I can't stand gramophones," Anton Pavlovich confessed sadly.

" Why ? "

" They speak and sing without feeling. Everything seems like a caricature—dead. Do you like photography ? "

It appeared that the lawyer was a passionate lover of photography; he began at once to speak of it with enthusiasm, completely uninterested, as Chekhov had subtly and truly noticed, in the gramophone, despite his admiration for that " amazing invention." And again I observed how there looked out of that uniform a living and rather amusing little man, whose feelings towards life were still those of a puppy hunting.

When Anton Pavlovich had seen him out, he said sternly:

" They are like pimples on the seat of justice— disposing of the fate of people."

And after a short silence:

" Crown Prosecutors must be very fond of fishing— especially for little fish."

.   .   .   .   .

He had the art of revealing everywhere and driving away banality, an art which is only possible to a man who demands much from life and which comes from a keen desire to see men simple, beautiful, harmonious. Banality always found in him a discerning and merciless judge.

Someone told in his presence how the editor of a popular magazine, who was always talking of the necessity of love and pity, had, for no reason at all, insulted a railway guard, and how he usually acted with extreme rudeness towards his inferiors.

" Well," said Anton Pavlovich with a gloomy smile, " but isn't he an aristocrat, an educated gentleman ? He studied at the seminary. His father wore the best shoes, and he wears patent-leather boots."

And in his tone there was something which at once made the " aristocrat " trivial and ridiculous.

" He's a very gifted man," he said of a certain journalist. " He always writes so nobly, humanely . . . lemonadely. Calls his wife a fool in public . . . the servants' rooms are damp and the maids constantly get rheumatics."

" Don't you like N. N., Anton Pavlovich ? "

" Yes, I do—very much. He's a pleasant fellow," Anton Pavlovich agrees, coughing. " He knows everything . . . reads a lot . . . he hasn't returned three of my books . . . he's absent-minded. To-day he will tell you that you're a wonderful fellow, and to-morrow he will tell somebody else that you cheat your servants, and that you have stolen from your mistress's husband his silk socks—the black ones with the blue stripes."

Someone in his presence complained of the heaviness and tediousness of the " serious " sections in thick monthly magazines.

"But you must not read those articles," said Anton Pavlovich. "They are friends' literature—written for friends. They are written by Messrs. Red, Black, and White. One writes an article; the other replies to it; and the third reconciles the contradictions of the other two. It is like playing whist with a dummy. Yet none of them asks himself what good it is to the reader."

Once a plump, healthy, handsome, well-dressed lady came to him and began to speak *à la Chekhov*:

"Life is so boring, Anton Pavlovich. Everything is so grey: people, the sea, even the flowers seem to me grey. . . . And I have no desires . . . my soul is in pain . . . it is like a disease."

"It is a disease," said Anton Pavlovich with conviction, "it is a disease; in Latin it is called *morbus fraudulentus*."

Fortunately, the lady did not seem to know Latin, or, perhaps, she pretended not to know it.

"Critics are like horse-flies which prevent the horse from ploughing," he said, smiling his wise smile. "The horse works, all its muscles drawn tight like the strings on a double-bass, and a fly settles on his flanks and tickles and buzzes . . . he has to twitch his skin and swish his tail. And what does the fly buzz about ? It scarcely knows itself; simply because it is restless and wants to proclaim: ' Look, I too am living on the earth. See, I can buzz, too, buzz about anything.' For twenty-five years I have read criticisms of my stories, and I don't remember a single remark of any value or one word of valuable advice. Only once Skabichevsky wrote something which made an impression on me   . . he said I would die in a ditch, drunk."

Nearly always there was an ironical smile in his grey eyes, but at times they became cold, sharp, hard; at such times a harder tone sounded in his soft, sincere voice, and then it appeared that this modest, gentle man, when he found it necessary, could rouse himself vigorously against a hostile force and would not yield.

But sometimes, I thought, there was in his attitude towards people a feeling of hopelessness, almost of cold, resigned despair.

" A Russian is a strange creature," he said once. " As in a sieve nothing remains in him. In his youth he fills himself greedily with anything which he comes across, and after thirty years nothing remains but a kind of grey rubbish. . . . In order to live well and humanly one must work—work with love and with faith. But we, we can't do it. An architect, having

built a couple of decent buildings, sits down to play
cards, plays all his life, or else is to be found somewhere behind the scenes of some theatre. A doctor,
if he has a practice, ceases to be interested in science,
and reads nothing but the *Medical Journal*, and at
forty seriously believes that all diseases have their
origin in catarrh. I have never met a single civil
servant who had any idea of the meaning of his work:
usually he sits in the metropolis or the chief town of
the province, and writes papers and sends them off to
Zmev or Smorgon for attention. But that those papers
will deprive someone in Zmev or Smorgon of freedom
of movement—of that the civil servant thinks as little
as an atheist of the tortures of hell. A lawyer who has
made a name by a successful defence ceases to care
about justice, and defends only the rights of property,
gambles on the Turf, eats oysters, figures as a con-
noisseur of all the arts. An actor, having taken two or
three parts tolerably, no longer troubles to learn his
parts, puts on a silk hat, and thinks himself a genius.
Russia is a land of insatiable and lazy people: they
eat enormously of nice things, drink, like to sleep in
the day-time, and snore in their sleep. They marry in
order to get their house looked after, and keep
mistresses in order to get prestige in society. Their
psychology is that of a dog: when they are beaten,
they whine shrilly and run into their kennels; when

petted, they lie on their backs with their paws in the air and wag their tails."

Pain and cold contempt sounded in these words. But, though contemptuous, he felt pity, and, if in his presence you abused anyone, Anton Pavlovich would immediately defend him.

" Why do you say that ? He is an old man . . . he's seventy." Or, " But he's still so young . . . it's only stupidity."

And, when he spoke like that, I never saw a sign of aversion in his face.

.   .   .   .   .

When a man is young, banality seems only amusing and unimportant, but little by little it possesses a man; it permeates his brain and blood like a poison or asphyxiating fumes; he becomes like an old, rusty signboard: something is painted on it, but what ?— You can't make out.

Anton Pavlovich in his early stories was already able to reveal in the dim sea of banality its tragic humour; one has only to read his " humorous " stories with attention to see what a lot of cruel and disgusting things, behind the humorous words and situations, had been observed by the author with sorrow and were concealed by him.

He was ingenuously shy; he would not say aloud

and openly to people: " Now do be more decent ";
he hoped in vain that they would themselves see how
necessary it was that they should be more decent.
He hated everything banal and foul, and he described the abominations of life in the noble language
of a poet, with the humorist's gentle smile, and behind
the beautiful form of his stories people scarcely
noticed the inner meaning, full of bitter reproach.

The dear public, when it reads his *Daughter of
Albion*, laughs and hardly realizes how abominable is
the well-fed squire's mockery of a person who is
lonely and strange to everyone and everything. In
each of his humorous stories I hear the quiet, deep
sigh of a pure and human heart, the hopeless sigh of
sympathy for men who do not know how to respect
human dignity, who submit without any resistance
to mere force, live like fish, believe in nothing but
the necessity of swallowing every day as much thick
soup as possible, and feel nothing but fear that
someone, strong and insolent, will give them a hiding.

No one understood as clearly and finely as Anton
Chekhov the tragedy of life's trivialities, no one
before him showed men with such merciless truth the
terrible and shameful picture of their life in the dim
chaos of bourgeois everyday existence.

His enemy was banality; he fought it all his life
long; he ridiculed it, drawing it with a pointed and

unimpassioned pen, finding the mustiness of banality even where at the first glance everything seemed to be arranged very nicely, comfortably, and even brilliantly—and banality revenged itself upon him by a nasty prank, for it saw that his corpse, the corpse of a poet, was put into a railway truck " For the Conveyance of Oysters."

That dirty green railway truck seems to me precisely the great, triumphant laugh of banality over its tired enemy; and all the " Recollections " in the gutter Press are hypocritical sorrow, behind which I feel the cold and smelly breath of banality, secretly rejoicing over the death of its enemy.

.   .   .   .   .

Reading Anton Chekhov's stories, one feels oneself in a melancholy day of late autumn, when the air is transparent and the outline of naked trees, narrow houses, greyish people, is sharp. Everything is strange, lonely, motionless, helpless. The horizon, blue and empty, melts into the pale sky, and its breath is terribly cold upon the earth, which is covered with frozen mud. The author's mind, like the autumn sun, shows up in hard outline the monotonous roads, the crooked streets, the little squalid houses in which tiny, miserable people are stifled by boredom and laziness and fill the houses with an unintelligible, drowsy bustle. Here, anxiously, like a grey mouse, scurries *The Darling*, the dear, meek woman who loves so slavishly and who can love so much. You can slap her cheek and she won't even dare to utter a sigh aloud, the meek slave. . . . And by her side is Olga of *The Three Sisters*: she too loves much, and submits with resignation to the caprices of the dissolute, banal wife of her good-for-nothing brother; the life of her sisters crumbles before her eyes, she weeps and cannot help anyone in anything, and she has not within her a single live, strong word of protest against banality.

And here is the lachrymose Ranevskaya and the other owners of " The Cherry Orchard," egotistical like children, with the flabbiness of senility. They missed the right moment for dying; they whine, seeing nothing of what is going on around them, understanding nothing, parasites without the power of again taking root in life. The wretched little student, Trofimov, speaks eloquently of the necessity of working—and does nothing but amuse himself, out of sheer boredom, with stupid mockery of Varya, who works ceaselessly for the good of idlers.

Vershinin dreams of how pleasant life will be in three hundred years, and lives without perceiving that everything around him is falling into ruin before his eyes; Solyony, from boredom and stupidity, is ready to kill the pitiable Baron Tonsenbach.

There passes before one a long file of men and women, slaves of their love, of their stupidity and idleness, of their greed for the good things of life; there walk the slaves of the dark fear of life; they straggle anxiously along, filling life with incoherent words about the future, feeling that in the present there is no place for them.

At moments out of the grey mass of them one hears the sound of a shot: Ivanov or Treplev has guessed what he ought to do and has died.

Many of them have nice dreams of how pleasant life will be in three hundred years, but it occurs to none of them to ask themselves who will make life pleasant if we only dream.

In front of that dreary, grey crowd of helpless people there passed a great, wise, and observant man; he looked at all these dreary inhabitants of his country, and, with a sad smile, with a tone of gentle but deep reproach, with anguish in his face and in his heart, in a beautiful and sincere voice, he said to them:

" You live badly, my friends. It is shameful to live like that."

REMINISCENCES OF
LEONID ANDREEV

Translated from the Russian by
KATHERINE MANSFIELD AND
S. S. KOTELIANSKY

H

This translation was made by Katherine
Mansfield and S. S. Koteliansky during
Katherine Mansfield's last stay in England,
in August and September 1922

REMINISCENCES
OF LEONID ANDREEV

In the spring of 1898 I read in the Moscow *Courier* a
story called " Bergamot and Garaska "—an Easter
story of the usual type. Written to appeal to the heart
of the holiday reader, it reminded him once again that
man is still capable, at certain moments and in certain
special circumstances, of a feeling of generosity, and
that at times enemies become friends, if only for a
short while, if only for a day.

Since Gogol's " Overcoat " Russian writers have
probably written several hundreds or even thousands
of such deliberately pathetic stories; they are, as it
were, the dandelions, which, scattered among the
superb flowers of genuine Russian literature, are
meant to brighten the beggarly life of the sick and
rigid Russian soul.[1]

But from that story there was borne to me the strong
breeze of a talent which reminded me in a way of
Pomyalovsky; again in the tone of the story one felt a

---

[1] It is quite likely that at that time my thoughts were different
from those I describe now, but it is not of interest to recall my
old thoughts.

roguish little smile of distrust of facts which the author concealed; that little smile easily reconciled one to inevitable, forced sentimentalism of Easter and Christmas literature.

I wrote the author a few lines about his story, and I received from L. Andreev an amusing answer; he wrote merry, unusual phrases in a singular handwriting, with half-printed letters, and amongst them stood out in particular relief a disingenuous but sceptical aphorism:

"To a well-fed man to be generous is as pleasant as to have coffee after dinner."

So began my acquaintance with Leonid Nicolaievich Andreev. In the summer I read some more of his short stories and light articles under his journalistic pseudonym of James Lynch, and noticed how quickly and boldly the individual talent of the new writer was developing.

In the autumn, on my way to the Crimea, at the Kursk railway station in Moscow, someone introduced us to each other. Dressed in an oldish overcoat, in a shaggy sheepskin hat tilted to one side, he looked like a young actor in an Ukrainian theatrical company. His handsome face struck me as not very mobile, but in the fixed glance of his dark eyes gleamed the smile which so pleasantly irradiated his stories and light articles. I don't remember his words, but they were unusual, and unusual also was the construction of his agitated speech. He spoke hurriedly, with a dullish, booming voice, with a little crisp cough, his words slightly choking him, while he waved his hands monotonously as though he were conducting. He appeared to me a healthy, sprite-like, cheery man, capable of supporting with a laugh the woes of this world. His excitement was pleasant.

"Let us be friends!" he said, pressing my hand.

I, too, was joyfully excited.

§

In the winter, on my way from the Crimea to Nijni, I stopped in Moscow, and there our relations rapidly assumed the character of a close friendship.

Seeing how little in touch he was with reality, how little interested in it, indeed—I was the more surprised by the power of his intuition, by the fertility of his imagination, by the grip of his fantasy. A single phrase, at times a single pointed word, was enough to start him off, and seizing the insignificant thing given him he would instantly develop it into a scene, anecdote, character, story.

"Who is S. ?" he asked about a certain author fairly popular at that time.

" A tiger out of a furrier's shop," I replied.

He laughs, and lowering his voice, as though communicating a secret, says hurriedly:

" You know, I must describe a man who has convinced himself that he is a hero, a tremendous destroyer of all that exists, and has become frightful to himself even—yes! Everybody believes him—so well has he deceived himself. But somewhere in his own corner—in real life—he is a mere miserable nonentity, is afraid of his wife or even of his cat."

So winding one word after another round the core of his flexible thought, he was always creating something unexpected and singular, easily and gaily.

The palm of one of his hands had been pierced by a bullet, his fingers were crooked; I asked him how it happened.

" An _équivoque_ of youthful romanticism," he replied. " You see, a man who has not tried to kill himself is very small beer."

Thereupon he sat down on the divan close to me, and in superb fashion related how once, when a youth, he had thrown himself under a goods train, but fortunately fell between the rails, and the train rushed over him and nearly stunned him.

There was something vague, unreal in the story, but he embellished it with an astonishingly vivid description of the sensations of a man over whom

hundreds of ton loads are moving with an iron
rumble. These sensations were familiar to me, too:
as a lad of about ten I used to lie down under a
ballast train, competing in audacity with my chums,
one of whom, the pointsman's son, played the game
with particular cool-headedness. It is an almost safe
amusement, provided the furnace of the locomotive is
raised high enough and the train is moving up hill,
not down hill, for then the brake-chains of the cars
are tightly stretched, and can't strike you, or, having
caught you, fling you on to the sleepers. For a few
seconds you experience an eerie sensation, you try to
press as flat and close to the ground as possible, and
with the exertion of your whole will to overcome the
passionate desire to stir, to raise your head. You feel
that the stream of iron and timber, rushing over you,
tears you off the ground and wants to drag you off
somewhere, and the rumble and grinding of the iron
rings as it were in your bones. Then, when the train
has passed, you still lie motionless for a minute or
more, powerless to rise, seeming to swim along after
the train; and it is as if your body stretches out end-
lessly, grows, becomes light, melts into air, and—the
next moment you will be flying above the earth. It is
very pleasant to feel all this.

" What fascinated you in such an absurd game ? "
asked Andreev.

I said that perhaps we were testing the power of our wills, by opposing to the mechanical motion of huge masses the conscious immobility of our puny little bodies.

" No," he replied, " that is too good; no child could think that."

Reminding him of how children love to " tread the cradle "—to gambol on the supple ice of a new-frozen pond or of a shallow river-edge, I said that they generally liked dangerous games.

" No, it can't be that, somehow. Nearly all children are afraid of the dark. . . . The poet said:

> 'There is delight in battle,
> And on the edge of a dark abyss;'

but that is merely ' fine words,' nothing more. I have a different idea, but I can't quite get at it."

And suddenly he started up as though touched by an inner fire.

" I must write a story about a man who all his life long, suffering madly, sought the truth. And, behold, truth appeared to him, but he shut his eyes, stopped his ears and said: ' I do not want thee, however fair thou mayst be, for my life, my torments, have kindled in my soul a hatred of thee.' What do you think ? "

I did not like the theme. He said, with a sigh:

" Yes, one must first answer wherein lies the truth
—in man or outside him ? According to you—it is in
man."

And he burst out into laughter:

" Then it is very bad, a very paltry affair."

§

There was scarcely a single fact, scarcely a single
problem, which Leonid Andreev and I looked at in
the same way, but innumerable differences did not
prevent us—for years—from regarding each other
with an intensity of interest and of consideration
which is seldom the result of even a long-standing
friendship. We were indefatigable in our discussions.
I remember we once sat uninterruptedly for over
twenty hours and drank several samovars of tea—
Leonid swallowed an incredible quantity of tea.

He was a wonderfully interesting talker, inex-
haustible, witty. Although his mind always mani-
fested a stubborn tendency to peer into the darkest
corners of the soul—nevertheless his thought was so
alert, so capriciously individual, that it readily took
grotesque and humorous forms. In a conversation
among friends he could use his sense of humour
flexibly and beautifully, but in his stories he unfortunately lost that capacity, so rare in a Russian.

Although he possessed a lively and sensitive imagination, he was lazy; he was much fonder of talking about literature than of creating it. The delight of martyr-like toil at night in stillness and solitude, seated before a white, clean sheet of paper, was almost impossible to him; he valued but little the joy of covering that sheet with the pattern of words.

" I write with difficulty. Writing is a strain on me," he would confess. " The nibs seem to me inconvenient, the process of writing too slow and even degrading. My thoughts flutter about like jackdaws in a fire, I soon tire of catching them and arranging them in proper order. Often this is what happens: I have written a word—and suddenly I get caught in a cobweb—for no reason I begin to think of geometry, algebra, and the teacher at my old school at Oriol— a very stupid man indeed. He often quoted the words of some philosopher: ' True wisdom is calm.' But I know that the best men on earth suffer torments of agitation. Curse calm wisdom! But what is there instead of it ? Beauty ? *Vivat ?* However, although I have not seen Venus in the original, she seems to me from her photographs a rather silly female. As a rule, pretty things are always rather stupid. Take, for instance, a peacock, a greyhound, a woman. . ."

§

Indifferent to facts of actuality, sceptical in his attitude to the mind and will of man—it would seem that the idea of laying down the law, of playing the teacher, ought not to have attracted him. That is a role inevitable for one who is familiar—much too familiar—with reality. But our very first conversation clearly indicated that, whilst possessing all the qualities of a superb artist, he wished to assume the pose of a thinker and of a philosopher as well. This seemed to me dangerous, almost hopeless, chiefly because his stock of knowledge was strangely poor. And one always felt as though he sensed the nearness of an invisible enemy, that he was arguing intensely with someone and wanted to subdue him.

Leonid was not fond of reading, and himself the maker of books—the creator of miracles—he looked upon old books distrustfully and heedlessly.

" A book to you is like a fetish to a savage," he would say. " That is because you have not rubbed holes in your breeches on the benches of a public school, because you have not come into contact with university learning. But to me the *Iliad*, Pushkin, and all the rest are beslavered by teachers, prostituted by constipated officials. *Sorrow through Knowledge*[1] is as

[1] A Play by Griboedov.

boring to me as Hall and Knight's arithmetic. I am as sick of *The Captain's Daughter* as I am of the little lady from the Tverskoy Boulevard."

I had heard these familiar words about the influence of the public school on one's attitude to literature too often, and they had long since sounded to me unconvincing, for one felt in them the prejudice begotten by Russian laziness. Much more original was Andreev when describing how the reviews and critical articles in the papers mutilate and maim books, treating them in the style of reports of street accidents.

" They are mills, they grind Shakespeare, the Bible —anything you like—into the dust of banality. I once read in a paper a critical article on *Don Quixote*, and I suddenly saw with horror that Don Quixote was an old man of my acquaintance, a director of the Court of Exchequer; he had a chronic cold in the nose, and a mistress, a girl from a confectionery shop, whom he called by the grand name of Millie, but in actual life—on the boulevards—she was known as Sonka Bladder. . . ."

But although he regarded knowledge and books lightly, heedlessly, and at times with hostility, he was always keenly interested in what I was reading. On one occasion, seeing in my room at the " Moscow Hotel " Alexey Ostrumov's book on Synesius, the Bishop of Ptolemais, he asked wonderingly:

" What do you want this for ? "

I told him about the queer half-pagan Bishop, and read a few lines from his work *In Praise of Baldness*. " What [asks Synesius] can be more bald yet what is more divine than the sphere ? "

This pathetic exclamation of the descendant of Hercules drove Leonid into a fit of laughter, but immediately wiping the tears from his eyes and still laughing he said:

" You know, it is a superb subject for a story about an unbeliever who, wishing to test the stupidity of believers, assumes a mask of saintliness, lives the life of a martyr, preaches a new doctrine of God—a very stupid doctrine—and so attains the love and admiration of thousands. Then he says to his disciples and followers: ' All this is rubbish.' But they need a faith, and so they kill him."

I was struck by his words. The point was that Synesius had expressed the same idea:

" If I were told that a Bishop must share the opinions of the people, I would reveal to all who I am. For what can there be in common between the rabble and philosophy? Divine truth must be hidden; the people need something quite different."

But I had not told Andreev of that idea, nor had I the opportunity of telling him about the unusual position of the unbaptized pagan philosopher in the role of Bishop of a Christian Church. When eventually I did so, he exclaimed triumphantly and laughing:

"There, you see—one does not need to be always reading in order to know and to understand."

§

Leonid was talented by nature, organically talented; his intuition was astonishingly keen. In all that touched on the dark side of life, the contradictions in the human soul, the rumblings in the domain of the instincts, he had eerie powers of divination. The instance of Bishop Synesius is not the only one, I could quote a score of such cases.

Thus, talking with him about various seekers after an unshakable belief, I related to him the contents of the MS. *Confession*, by the priest Apollonov—a work by one of the unknown martyrs of thought which had called forth Leo Tolstoy's *Confession*. I told him what I had observed personally of men of dogmatic beliefs: they often appear voluntary prisoners of a blind, unyielding faith, and the more they actively defend its validity the more despairingly they doubt it.

Andreev mused for a while, slowly stirring his glass of tea; then he said, smiling:

"It is strange to me that you understand this; you

speak like an atheist, but you think as a believer. If you die before me I will inscribe on your gravestone: ' Crying to others to worship reason he himself secretly jeered at its impotence.' "

And in a couple of minutes, leaning on my shoulder, glancing into my eyes with the dilated pupils of his dark eyes, he said in an undertone:

" I shall write about a parson, you will see ! This, my dear fellow, I shall do well ! "

And threatening someone with his finger, vigorously rubbing his temples, he smiled:

" To-morrow I am going home and shall begin it ! I have even got the opening sentence: ' Among people he was lonely, for he had a glimpse of a great mystery.' . . ."

Next day he went away to Moscow, and in a week's time—not more—he wrote to me that he was working on the parson, and that his work was going smoothly " as on snow-shoes." Thus he always caught in flight anything that answered the needs of his spirit that was in contact with the most acute and tormenting mysteries of life.

§

The noisy success of his first book filled him to overflowing with youthful joy. He came to me at Nijni—

I

happy, in a brand new tobacco-coloured suit; the front of his stiffly starched shirt was adorned with a rakishly bright tie, and on his feet he had yellow boots.

" I tried to find straw-coloured gloves, but a lady in the shop at Kuznetski warned me that straw colour was no longer the fashion. I suspect that she told a fib. The truth was she valued the freedom of her heart too much to risk becoming convinced of my irresistible attractiveness in straw-coloured gloves. But, between ourselves, I can tell you that all this magnificence is uncomfortable; a blouse is much better."

And suddenly, hugging my shoulders, he said:

" I want to write a hymn, you know. I don't yet see—to whom or to what; but a hymn it must be! Something Schillerian, eh ? Something grand, sonorous—boom-m! "

I chaffed him about it.

" Well! " he exclaimed merrily. " Is not Ecclesiastes right when he says: ' Even a rotten life is better than a good death.' Although he puts it rather differently, something about a lion and a dog: ' For domestic purposes a bad dog is more useful than a nice lion.' Well, what do you think: could Job have read the Book of Ecclesiastes ? "

Intoxicated with the wine of joy he dreamt of a

journey on the Volga in a good boat, of walking to the Crimea.

" I'll drag you off, too. Otherwise you will build yourself in among these old bricks," he said, pointing to the books.

His happiness resembled the lively and comfortable state of a baby which has been hungry too long, and now thinks it has eaten enough to last for ever.

We sat on a wide divan, in a little room, drank red wine; Andreev took down from the shelf a note-book of poems:

" May I ? " he asked, and began reading aloud:

> Columns of coppery firs,
> The monotonous sound of the sea.

" It is the Crimea ? Now, I can't write poems, and I have no desire to. I like ballads best. As a rule:

> I love all that is new,
> Romantic, nonsensical,
> Like the poet
> Of olden times.

" I believe that is a song in the musical comedy *The Green Island*:

> And the trees are moaning
> Like verses unrhymed.

" That I like. But—tell me—why do you write poems ? It does not suit you at all. After all, whatever you may think, verse is an artificial business."

Then we composed parodies of Skitalez:

> I'll grasp a huge log
> In my mighty hand,
> And all of you—unto the seventh
>   generation—
> I will knock down flat!
> Moreover I will stupefy you—
> Hurrah! Tr-r-remble! I am glad—
> I'll dash Kasbeck on your heads,
> I'll bring down Ararat upon you!

He laughed as he went on composing verse after verse of delightful, amusing parodies. But suddenly bending towards me, with a glass of wine in his hand, he began in a low voice and gravely:

" I read recently an amusing anecdote. In a certain English town there stands a memorial to Robert Burns, the poet. But there is no inscription on the memorial to inform you to whom it is erected. At the foot of it a boy was selling newspapers. A certain author came up to him and said: ' I'll buy a paper from you if you'll tell me whose statue this is.' ' Robert Burns,' the boy replied. ' Splendid! ' said the author. ' Now I'll buy all your papers if you'll tell me why this memorial was erected to Robert Burns.' The boy replied: ' Because he is dead.' How do you like it ? "

I did not like it much; I was always seriously perturbed by Leonid's sharp and sudden fluctuations of mood.

§

Fame to him was not merely " a bright patch on the bard's old rags "—he wanted a great deal of it, he wanted it greedily and he made no secret of his desires. He said:

" When I was only fourteen I said to myself: I shall be famous, or life won't be worth living. I am not afraid of telling you that all that has been done before my time does not seem to me to be better than what I myself can do. If you take that for conceit, you are wrong. Yes! Don't you see that this must be the basic conviction of anyone who does not want to place himself in the impersonal ranks of the millions of others. Indeed, the conviction of one's uniqueness must—and can—serve as the source of creative power. First let us say to ourselves: We are not like all the others, and already we are on the way to prove this to all the rest as well."

" In a word, you are a baby which does not want to feed at its nurse's breast."

" Just so! I want the milk of my soul only. Man needs love and attention, or that people should fear him. This even peasants realize, when they put on the mask of a sorcerer. Happiest of all are those who are loved with fear, as Napoleon was."

" Have you read his *Memoirs* ? "

" No. I don't need to."

He winked at me, smiling:

" I, too, keep a diary and I know how it is done. Memoirs, Confessions and suchlike are the excrements of the soul that is poisoned by bad food."

He loved such sayings, and when they were successful he was sincerely delighted. Despite his gravitation towards pessimism, there was in him something ineradicably childish—for instance, his childishly naïve boasting about his verbal agility, of which he made much better use in conversation than on paper.

Once I told him about a woman who prided herself to such a degree on her " honest " life and took so much trouble to convince all and sundry of her inaccessibility that those who surrounded her gasped from weariness, and either rushed headlong away from this model of virtue, or hated her to the verge of frenzy.

Andreev listened, smiled and suddenly said:

" I am an honest woman, I am. I have no need to clean my nails, eh ? "

In these words, with almost perfect exactness he defined the character and even the habits of the creature of whom I was speaking—the woman was careless in her person. I told him this. He was delighted, and with childish sincerity began to boast:

"My dear fellow, I am myself surprised at times to find how cleverly and pointedly I can in two or three words seize the very essence of a fact or of a character."

And he delivered a long speech in praise of himself; but—sensible man that he was—he realized that this was a trifle ridiculous, and he ended his tirade with a touch of buffoonery.

"In time I shall develop my capacity as a genius to such an extent that I shall be able to define in a single word the meaning of the whole life of a man, of a nation, of an epoch. . . ."

Yet the critical attitude towards himself was not particularly strongly developed in him, and this at times greatly spoiled his work and his life.

§

In every one of us, to my thinking, live and struggle embryos of several personalities. These dispute between themselves until, in the struggle, there is developed the embryo which is the strongest and most capable of adapting itself to the various reactions to impressions which form the final spiritual character of a man, thus creating a more or less complete psychical individuality.

Strangely and to his own torment Leonid split into

two: in one and the same week he could sing " Hosannah " to the world, and pronounce " Anathema " against it.

This was not an external contradiction between the bases of his character and the habits or demands of his profession; no, in both cases he felt equally sincerely. And the more loudly he proclaimed Hosannah, the more powerfully resounded the echo "Anathema."

He said:

" I hate individuals who refuse to walk on the sunny side of the street for fear that their faces may be burnt or their jackets faded—I hate all those who for dogmatic motives hamper the free, capricious play of their inner ego."

Once he wrote a rather caustic article on the people of the shady side, and immediately after this —on the occasion of Émile Zola's death from gas fumes—engaged in a vigorous attack on the barbarous asceticism at that time fairly popular among the intelligentzia. But talking to me about that attack he declared suddenly:

" And yet, you know, my opponent is more consistent than I am: a writer ought to live like a homeless tramp. Maupassant's yacht is an absurdity! "

He was not joking. We had an argument. I maintained: the more varied the needs of man, the more

eager he is for the joys of life, however paltry, the
quicker develops the culture of the body and of the
spirit. He retorted: No, Tolstoy is right, culture is
rubbish, it only maims the free growth of the soul.

" ' Attachment to things,' " he would say, " is the
fetishism of savages, idolatry. Don't make an idol for
yourself, if you do you are rotten—that is the truth!
Make a book to-day, and to-morrow make a machine.
Yesterday you made a book, and you have already
forgotten about it. We must learn to forget."

And I said: " It is necessary to remember that each
thing is the embodiment of the human spirit, and
often the inner value of a thing is more significant
than man."

" That is worship of dead matter," he exclaimed.

" In it is embodied immortal thought."

" What is thought ? Its impotence makes it double-
faced and disgusting."

We argued more and more often, more and more
intensely. The sharpest point of difference was our
attitude to thought.

To me—thought is the source of all that exists, out
of thought arose everything that is seen and felt by
man; even in the consciousness of its impotence to
solve the " accursed questions " thought is majestic
and noble.

I feel that I live in the atmosphere of thought, and,

seeing the great and grand things that have been created by it—I believe that its impotence is temporary. Perhaps I am romancing and exaggerate the creative power of thought; but this is so natural in Russia, in a country where there is no spiritual synthesis, in a country paganly sensual, monstrously cruel.

Leonid regarded thought as a " wicked trick played on man by the devil "; it seemed to him false and hostile. Luring man to the abysses of inexplicable mysteries it deceives him, it leaves him in painful and impotent loneliness in face of all that is mysterious, and itself vanishes.

Equally irreconcilably did we differ in our views on man, the source of thought, its furnace. To me man is always the conqueror, even when he is mortally wounded and dying. Splendid is his longing to know himself and to know Nature: and although his life is a torment, he is ever widening its bounds, creating with his thoughts wise science, marvellous art. I felt that I did sincerely and actively love man—him who is at present alive and working side by side with me, and him, too, the sensible, the good, the strong, who will follow after in the future. To Andreev man appeared poor in spirit, a creature interwoven of irreconcilable contradictions of instinct and intellect, for ever deprived of the possibility of attaining inner harmony.

All his works are " vanity of vanities," decay and self-deception. And above all he is the slave of death and all his life long he walks, dragging its chain.

§

It is very difficult to speak of a man whom you know and know profoundly.

That sounds like a paradox; but it is true: when the mysterious thrill that emanates from the flame of another's ego is felt by you, agitates you—you fear to touch with your oblique clumsy words the invisible rays of the soul that is dear to you; you fear lest you express things wrongly. You don't want to mutilate what you feel and what is almost indefinable in words; you dare not enclose in your constricted speech that which is the essence of another, even though it be universally valid, of human value.

It is much easier and simpler to speak of what you feel less vividly. In such cases you can add a great deal, indeed anything you like, for yourself.

I think that I comprehended Leonid Andreev clearly: to be more exact, I saw that he was treading a path overhanging a precipice, a precipice that leads to the slough of madness, a precipice at the mere contemplation of which the sight of the mind is extinguished.

Great was the force of his imagination; but not-
withstanding the continuous and strained attention
which he gave to the humiliating mystery of death,
he could not imagine anything beyond it, nothing
majestic or comforting—he was after all too much of a
realist to invent comfort for himself even though he
wished it.

This preference of his for treading the path over
the void was what above all kept us apart. I had
passed through Leonid's mood long before—and
through natural human pride, it became organically
revolting and humiliating to me to reflect on death.
The time had come when I said to myself: while that
which feels and thinks in me is alive, death dare not
touch that power.

I once told Leonid of how I had once to go through
a hard time of " the prisoner's dream of life beyond
the bounds of his prison," of " stony darkness," of
" immobility for ever poised "; he jumped up from
the divan, and pacing the room, waving his maimed
hand, he said hurriedly, indignantly, gasping for
breath:

" It is cowardice, my dear fellow, to shut the book
without reading it to the end! In the book is your
indictment, in it you are denied, don't you see ? You
are denied along with everything there is in you, with
your humanism, socialism, æsthetics, love—isn't all

this nonsense according to the book ? It is ridiculous and pitiable: you have been sentenced to death—for what ? And you, pretending that you are not aware of the fact, play about with little flowers, deceiving yourself and others—silly little flowers! . . ."

I pointed out to him the futility of protesting against an earthquake; I argued that protests cannot in the least affect the tremors of the earth's crust—all this merely angered him.

We talked in Petersburg, in the autumn, in an empty, depressing room on the fifth floor. The city was enveloped in a thick mist; in its grey mass the ghostly, rainbow globes of the street lamps hung motionless like huge bubbles. Through the thin cotton wool of the mist nonsensical sounds rose up from the well of the street. Wearisome above all else were the hooves of the horses drumming on the wooden blocks of the road.

Leonid went and stood by the window, with his back to me. I realized keenly that at that moment he hated me as a man who walked the earth more easily and more freely than he, because he had thrown from his shoulders a humiliating and useless burden.

Even before this I had felt in him sharp spurtings of anger against me, but I can't say that this offended me, although it did alarm me; I understood—in my own way certainly—the source of his anger, and how

life was hard on this rarely gifted man, dear to me
and—at that time—my intimate friend.

There, below, the fire brigade dashed along noisily.
Leonid came up to me, threw himself on the divan
and suggested:

" Shall we drive to see the fire ? "

" In Petersburg a fire isn't interesting."

He agreed.

" True, but in the provinces, in Oriol, say, when
streets of wooden buildings are burning and the
people dash about like moths—it is nice! And
pigeons over the cloud of smoke—have you ever seen
that ? "

Hugging my shoulders he said, smiling:

" You see everything—the devil take you! ' Stony
emptiness '—that is very good. Stony darkness and
emptiness! You do understand the mood of the
captive. . . ."

And butting my side with his head:

" At times I hate you for this as I do a beloved
woman who is cleverer than myself."

I said I felt this, and that only a minute before he
had hated me.

" Yes," he agreed, nestling his head on my knees.
" Do you know why ? I wish you were aching with
my pain, then we should be nearer to one another—
you really do know how lonely I am! "

Yes, he was very lonely, but at times it appeared to me that he jealously guarded his loneliness, it was dear to him as the source of his fantastic inspirations and the fertile soil of his originality.

"You lie when you say that scientific thought satisfies you," he said sternly, looking darkly at the ceiling with scared eyes. " Science, my dear fellow, is only mysticism dealing with facts: nobody knows anything—that's the truth. And the problem: how I think and why I think, is the source of man's greatest torment—this is the most terrible truth! Come, let's go off somewhere, please. . . ."

Whenever he touched on the problem of the mechanism of thinking, he became most agitated. And frightened.

We put on our coats, descended into the mist, and for a couple of hours swam in it on the Nevsky like eels at the bottom of a slimy river. Then we sat in a café and three girls pressed themselves on us, one of them a graceful Estonian who called herself Elfrida. Her face was stony; she looked at Andreev out of large, grey, lustreless eyes with eerie gravity while she drank a greenish venomous liqueur out of a coffee cup. It smelt of burnt leather.

Leonid drank cognac, rapidly got tipsy, became riotously witty, made the girls laugh by his surprisingly amusing and ingenious jokes, and at last decided to drive to the girls' flat—they were very insistent on this. To leave Leonid was impossible; whenever he began drinking something uncanny awoke in him, a revengeful need of destruction, the fury of " the captured beast."

I went with him. We bought wine, fruit, sweets, and somewhere in the Razezhaya Street, in the corner of a dirty courtyard, blocked up with casks and timber, on the second floor of a wooden outbuilding, in two tiny rooms, the walls wretchedly and pathetically adorned with picture postcards—we began to drink.

Before he got to the state in which he would lose consciousness Leonid always became dangerously and wonderfully excited, his brain boiled up riotously, his imagination flared, his speech became almost intolerably brilliant.

One of the girls, plump, soft, and agile as a mouse, told us, almost with rapture, how the Assistant Crown Prosecutor had bitten her leg above the knee; she evidently considered the lawyer's action the most significant event of her life. She showed the scar left by the bite and, choking with agitation, her little glassy eyes shining with joy, said:

" He was awfully gone on me, it's quite frightening to remember it! He bit, you know, and he has a false tooth—and it stuck in my skin! "

This girl quickly got drunk, tumbled down in a corner of the couch, and fell asleep, snoring. The full-bodied, thick-haired, chestnut-coloured girl, with sheepish eyes and monstrously long arms, played the guitar, and Elfrida deliberately undressed until she was stark naked, moved the bottles and plates on to the floor, jumped on the table and danced silently, wriggling like a serpent without taking her eyes from Leonid. Then she began to sing in an unpleasantly thick voice, with angrily dilated eyes, and now and then, as though broken in half, she bent over Andreev. He kissed her knees, repeating the words he had caught up of the strange foreign song, while he nudged me with his elbow and said:

" She understands something, look at her, do you see ? She understands! "

At moments Leonid's excited eyes seemed to go blind; growing still darker they sank deeper, as if in an attempt to peer inside his brain.

Grown tired the Estonian jumped from the table to the bed, stretched herself, her mouth open, stroking with her palms her little breasts, sharp as a she-goat's.

Leonid said:

" The highest and deepest sensation in life accessible to us is the spasm of the sexual act—yes, yes! Perhaps the earth, just like this b—— here, is rushing

K

about in the desert of the universe expecting me to impregnate her with the realization of the purpose of life, and I myself, with all that is marvellous in me, am only a spermatozoon."

I suggested to him that we should go home.

" Go, I will stay here. . . ."

I could not leave him—he was already very drunk, and he had a good deal of money on him. He sat down on the bed, stroking the girl's finely shaped legs, and began in an amusing way to tell her he loved her. She never let her eyes leave his face, her head resting on her hands.

" The baron has only to eat horse-radish to grow wings," Leonid said.

" No, it isn't true," the girl said gravely.

" I told you she understands something! " exclaimed Leonid in drunken joy. In a few minutes he came out of the room. I gave the girl money and asked her to persuade Leonid to go for a drive. She instantly agreed, jumped up and began quickly to dress.

" I am afraid of him," she murmured. " Men like him pull out revolvers."

The girl who played the guitar fell asleep, sitting on the floor near the couch where her friend slept and snored.

The Estonian was dressed by the time Leonid returned. He began making a row and shouted:

" I don't want to go! Let there be a feast of the flesh! "

And he attempted to undress the girl again; but struggling with him, she gazed so stubbornly into his eyes that her look tamed Leonid, and he agreed:

" Let us go! "

But he wanted to put on the lady's hat *à la Rembrandt* and had already plucked out the feathers.

" You'll pay for the hat ? " the girl asked in a business-like fashion.

Leonid raised his brows and burst into laughter.

" The hat settles it! Hooray! "

In the street we took a cab and drove through the mist. It was still not late, about midnight. The Nevsky with its huge beads of lamps looked like a road going down hill into a hollow; round the lamps flitted wet particles of dust, in the grey dampness black fishes swam, standing on their tails, the hemispheres of the umbrellas seemed to draw people up— all was very ghostly, strange and sad.

In the open air Andreev became completely drunk. He fell into a doze, swaying from side to side. The girl whispered to me:

" I'll get out. Shall I ? "

And jumping from my knees into the liquid mud of the street she disappeared.

At the end of the Kamennostrovsky Prospect
Leonid asked, opening his eyes with a start:

" Are we driving ? I want to go to a pub. You
sent her away ? "

" She went away."

" You are lying! You are cunning, so am I. I left
the room in order to see what you would do. I stood
behind the door and heard you urging her to make
me go for a drive. You behaved innocently and
nobly. When it comes to the point, you are a bad
man. You drink a lot but don't get drunk, and
because of this your children will be dipsomaniacs.
My father also drank a great deal and did not get
drunk, and I am an alcoholic."

Then we sat and smoked in the " Strelka," under
the stupid bubble of the mist, and when the light of
our cigarettes flared up we could see our overcoats
covered with dim glass beads of dampness turning to
grey.

Leonid spoke with boundless frankness, and it was
not the frankness of a drunken man. His mind was
scarcely affected until the moment when the poison
of the alcohol completely stopped the working of his
brain.

" You have done and are doing a great deal for
me—even to-day, I quite understand. If I had
remained with the girls it would have ended badly

for someone. Just so. But it is just because of this that I don't love you, precisely because of this. You prevent me from being myself. Leave me! I want to expand. Perhaps you are the hoop on the cask; you will go away and the cask will fall to pieces; but let it fall to pieces—do you understand? Nothing should be restrained; let everything be destroyed. Perhaps the true meaning of life consists indeed in the destruction of something which we don't know, of everything that has been thought out and made by us."

His dark eyes were fixed sternly on the grey mass around and above him; now and then he turned them towards the wet, leaf-strewn ground, and he stamped his feet as though testing the firmness of the earth.

" I don't know what you think, but what you always say is not the expression of your faith, of your prayer. You say that all the forces of life spring from the violation of equilibrium. But you yourself are indeed seeking for an equilibrium, for some kind of harmony, and are urging me to seek for the same thing; whereas—on your own showing—equilibrium is death!"

I said I was not urging him to anything, I had no wish to urge him, but his life was dear to me, his health was dear, his work.

" It is only my work that pleases you—my external self, but not I myself, not that which I cannot incarnate in work. You stand in my way and in everybody's way. Into the mud with you! "

He leant on my shoulder and, peering into my face, with a smile he went on:

" You think I am drunk and don't realize that I am talking nonsense ? I simply want to make you angry. You are a rare friend, I know, and you are stupidly disinterested, and I am a *farceur* begging for attention, like a beggar who shows his sores."

This he said not for the first time, and I recognized a grain of truth in it. Or rather, a cleverly contrived explanation of certain peculiarities of his character.

" I, my dear fellow, am a decadent, a degenerate, a sick man. But Dostoevsky was also a sick man, as are all great men. There's a book, I don't remember by whom, about genius and insanity; it proves that genius is a psychical disease! That little book has spoiled me. If I had not read it I should be a simpler man. And now, I know that I am almost a genius, but I am not sure whether I am sufficiently insane. Do you understand ? I pretend to myself to be insane in order to convince myself of my talent—do you see ? "

I burst out laughing. This seemed to me a poor invention, and therefore untrue.

When I said so, he also burst out laughing, and
suddenly, with a flexible movement of his soul, with
the agility of an acrobat, he leapt into the tone of a
humorist:

" Ah! Where is a pub, the temple of literary worship ? Talented Russians must necessarily converse
in pubs. That is the tradition, and without it the
critics won't admit talent."

We sat in a night tavern for cabmen in damp,
smoky stuffiness. The " waiters " raced about the
dirty room angrily and wearily, drunken men swore
" astronomically," terrible prostitutes screamed, and
one of them bared her left breast—huge and yellow—
put it on a plate, presented it to us, saying:

" Won't you buy a pound ? "

" I love shamelessness," said Leonid. " In cynicism
I feel the sadness, almost the despair of man, who
realizes that he can't—do you understand ?—that he
can't help being a beast. He wants not to be one, but
he can't! Do you understand ? "

He drank strong, almost black tea. I knew that he
liked it so and that it sobered him, and I purposely
ordered it strong. Sipping the tarry bitter liquid, his
eyes probing the puffy faces of the drunkards, Leonid
spoke uninterruptedly:

" With women I am cynical. It's the more truthful
way—and they love it. It's better to be a consummate

sinner than a righteous man who can't puff himself
up into a state of complete saintliness."

He glanced round, was silent for a while, and
said:

" Here it is as boring as an Ecclesiastical Council! "
This made him laugh.

" I've never been at an Ecclesiastical Council, it
must be something like a fishpond. . . ."

The tea sobered him. We left the tavern. The mist
thickened, the opalescent globes of the street lamps
melted like ice.

" I should like some fish," said Leonid, as he leant
his elbows on the parapet of the bridge across the
Neva, and continued with animation: " You know
my way ? Probably children think like that. A child
will pitch on a word and begin to pick out words that
rhyme to it: fish, dish, butter, gutter—but I can't
write verse."

After thinking for a while he added:

" Makers of children's alphabets think like that. . . ."

Again we sat in a tavern treating ourselves to a fish
solianka; Leonid was saying that the " decadents "
had invited him to contribute to their review *Vyessy*.

" I shan't accept, I don't like them. With them I
feel there is no body behind their words. They
' intoxicate ' themselves with words, as Balmont is
fond of saying. He too is talented and—sick."

On another occasion, I remember, he said of the *Scorpion* group:

" They outrage Schopenhauer, and I love him, and therefore hate them."

But on his lips, this was too strong a word—to hate was beyond him, he was too gentle for that. Once he showed me in his diary " words of hatred," but they turned out to be merely humorous, and he himself laughed heartily at them.

I saw him to his hotel in a cab, and put him to bed. But when I called in the afternoon, I learned that immediately after I left he got up, dressed, and disappeared. I searched for him the whole day, but could not find him.

He drank continuously for four days and then went away to Moscow.

§

He had an unpleasant way of testing the sincerity of people's mutual relations. He did it like this: suddenly he would ask, as if by the way, " Do you know what Z. said about you ? " Or he would let you know, " S. says of you. . . ." And with a dark glance he would look into your eyes as if to test you.

Once I said to him: " Look here, if you go on like

that you will end by setting all your friends against one another!"

"What of it?" he replied, "if they quarrel for trifles like that, it only shows that their relations were not sincere."

"Well, what do you want?"

"Stability, a sort of monumental firmness, beauty of relationship. Each one of us ought to realize how delicate is the lace of the soul, how tenderly and warily it should be regarded. A certain romanticism is needed in the relations between friends; it used to exist in Pushkin's circle, and I envy them it. Women are sensitive only to eroticism. The woman's gospel is the *Decameron*."

But in half an hour's time he scoffed at his view of women, as he gave a droll description of a conversation between an erotomaniac and a public-school girl.

He could not stand Artsibashev and at times scoffed at him with crude hostility just for his one-sided presentations of woman as exclusively sensual.

§

Once he told me this story. When he was about eleven he saw, somewhere in a wood or park, the deacon kissing a young girl.

"They kissed one another, and both cried," he

said, lowering his voice and shrinking. Whenever he told anything intimate, his limp muscles became strained and keyed up.

" The young girl, you see, was so slim and fragile, little legs like matches; the deacon—fat, the cassock on his belly greasy and shiny. I already knew why people kissed, but it was the first time I saw them crying when they kissed, and I thought it funny. The deacon's beard got caught on the girl's open blouse. He began wriggling his head. I whistled in order to frighten them—but got frightened myself and ran away. On the evening of that very same day I felt myself in love with the daughter of our magistrate, a girl of ten. I touched her: she had no breasts. So there was nothing to kiss, and she was not fit for love. Then I fell in love with a neighbour's maid, a short-legged girl, with white eyebrows, with enormous breasts—the blouse on her bosom was as greasy as the cassock on the deacon's belly. I approached her very resolutely, and she as resolutely pulled my ear. But this did not prevent me from loving her. She seemed to me a beauty, and the longer I knew her the more beautiful she seemed. It was almost torture and very sweet. I saw many really beautiful girls and in my mind I well understood that my beloved was a monster compared with them, and yet to me she remained the fairest of all. This knowledge made me happy; nobody could love as I did that fat hussy with her white eyebrows and white eyelashes. Nobody —do you understand ?—could see in her one fairer than the fairest! "

He told this superbly, saturating his account with delightful humour, which I cannot reproduce. What a pity that he who in conversation was such a master of humour neglected or was afraid to enrich his stories with its play. Evidently he was afraid of spoiling the dark tones of his pictures with the varied colours of humour.

When I said it was a pity that he had forgotten how well he succeeded in creating out of the short-legged maid the first beauty in the world, that he no longer wished to extract the golden veins of beauty from the dirty mine of reality, he screwed up his eyes, comically and slyly, saying:

" See what a sweet tooth you have got! No, I am not going to pamper you, you romantics. . . ."

It was impossible to persuade him it was just he who was the romantic.

§

In his *Collected Works*, which he presented to me in 1915, Leonid wrote:

" Beginning with *Bergamot* in the *Courier*, all that is

contained here has been written, has passed before
your eyes, Alexei: it is to a large extent the history
of our relations."

This, unfortunately, is true; unfortunately, because
I think it would have been better for Andreev had he
not introduced " the history of our relations " into
his stories. But he did it too readily, and in his haste
to " refute " my views he thereby spoiled his whole.
It seemed it was just in my personality that he had
embodied his invisible enemy.

" I have written a story which you are sure not
to like," he once said to me. " Shall we read
it ? "

We read it. I liked the story very much, save for a
few details.

" That's a trifle, that I'll correct," he said with
animation, pacing the room, shuffling with his
slippers. Then he sat down by my side and throwing
back his hair he glanced into my eyes.

" Well, I know, I feel that you were sincere in
praising that story. But I can't understand how it can
please you."

" There are many things on earth which don't
please me; yet, so far as I can see, they are none the
worse for it."

" Reasoning like that you can't be a revolutionary."

" Now, do you look upon a revolutionary as

Nechaev did, who held that a revolutionary is not a man ? "

He embraced me, laughed:

" You don't properly understand yourself. But, look here, when I wrote *Thought* I had you in my mind. Alexei Savelov is you. There is one phrase there: ' Alexei was not talented '—this perhaps was wrong on my part, but with your stubbornness you so irritate me at times that you seem to me without talent. It was wrong of me to have written it, wasn't it ? "

He was agitated, he even blushed.

I calmed him, saying that I did not consider myself an Arab steed, but only a dray-horse. I knew that I owed my success not so much to my inborn talent as to my capacity for work, my love of work.

" You are a strange man," he said softly, interrupting my words, and suddenly, changing the tone of the conversation, he began musingly to speak of himself, of the agitations of his soul. He lacked the unpleasant general Russian habit of confessing and of doing penance. But at times he managed to speak of himself with manly frankness, even severity, yet without losing his self-respect. And this was pleasant in him.

" You understand," he said, " every time I write something that particularly agitates me I feel as though a crust had fallen from my soul; I see myself

more clearly and I see that I am more talented than
the thing written. Take *Thought*. I expected it would
astonish you, and now I myself see that it is, essentially, a story with a purpose, which, even so, misses
the mark."

He jumped to his feet, and shaking back his hair
half jokingly declared:

" I'm afraid of you, you rascal! You are stronger
than I. I don't want to submit to you."

And again gravely:

" Something is lacking in me, my dear fellow.
Something very important—eh? What do you
think ? "

I thought that he treated his talent with unpardon-
able carelessness and that he lacked knowledge.

" One must study, read, go to Europe. . . ."

He waved his hand:

" It isn't that. One must find a god for oneself and
learn to believe in his wisdom."

As usual we began arguing. After one such argument he sent me the proofs of his story, *The Wall*, and
with reference to his *Ghosts* he said to me:

" The lunatic who knocks is myself, and the
energetic Yegor is you. You really possess confidence
in your powers; that is your obsession and the
obsession of all your fellow romantics, idealizers of
reason, uprooted from life by their dream."

§

The outcry aroused by his story *The Abyss* unnerved him. People ever ready to cater for the gutter Press began writing all sorts of unpleasant things about Andreev, going so far in their calumnies as to approach absurdity. Thus a certain poet announced in a Kharkov paper that Andreev and his fiancée bathed with no costumes on.

Leonid plaintively asked:

" What does he think then, that one must bathe in a frock-coat ? And he lies, too. I did not bathe either with a fiancée or solo. I have not bathed for a whole year—there was no river to bathe in. Look here, I have made up my mind to print and have posted on the hoardings a humble request to readers —a brief one:

> Yours is bliss
> Who don't read *Abyss*!

He was excessively, almost morbidly, attentive to his Press notices, and always, with sadness or with irritation, complained of the barbarous coarseness of the critics and reviewers; once he even wrote to the Press to complain of the hostile attitude adopted towards him personally.

" You should not do this," he was advised.

" Yes, I must. Otherwise these people, in their zeal to reform me, will cut off my ears or scald me with boiling water. . . ."

§

He suffered cruelly from hereditary alcoholism; his malady would manifest itself at comparatively rare intervals, but nearly always in a very aggravated form. He fought against it, the struggle cost him enormous efforts, but, at times, falling into despair, he scoffed at his efforts.

" I'll write a story about a man who, from his youth onwards, was for twenty-five years afraid to drink a thimbleful of vodka. Because of this he lost a multitude of splendid hours in life, he spoilt his career, and died in his prime through having cut his corn unsuccessfully or run a splinter into his finger."

And indeed, when he came to see me at Nijni, he brought with him the MS. of that very story.

§

In Nijni Leonid met at my house Father Feodor Vladimirsky, the archpriest of the town of Arzamas, who subsequently became a member of the Second

L

State Duma—a remarkable man. Some time I will
try and write about him fully, and meanwhile I find
it necessary briefly to outline the chief deed of his life.

The town of Arzamas, almost from the time of Ivan
the Terrible, obtained its water from ponds, where,
in the summer, swam corpses of drowned cats, rats,
fowls, dogs, while in the winter, under the ice, the
water became tainted, and had a disgusting smell.
Father Feodor, having made it his object to supply the
town with wholesome water, spent twelve years in
investigating personally the hidden waters around
Arzamas. Every summer, year in and year out, he
rose at dawn and wandered like a sorcerer about the
fields and woods, observing where the ground "per-
spired." And after long labour he found hidden
subsoil springs, traced their course, canalized them,
conducted them to a forest hollow a couple of miles
from the town; and having obtained for a population
of ten thousand over a hundred thousand gallons of
superb spring water, proposed to the town the laying
down of a water supply.

The town had a sum of money bequeathed to it by a
merchant to be used either for the laying down of a
water supply or for the founding of a credit bank.
The tradespeople and the authorities, who employed
horses to carry the water in barrels from remote
springs outside the town, had no need of a water

supply, and using all means to hinder the work of Father Feodor, tried to get hold of the capital for the establishment of a credit bank; while the unimportant inhabitants swallowed the tainted water of the ponds, indifferent and passive, in conformity with their immemorial custom. Thus, having found water, Father Feodor was compelled to carry on a long and tedious struggle with the stubborn selfishness of the rich and the villainous stupidity of the poor.

When I arrived at Arzamas under police surveillance[1] I found him at the end of his work of gathering together the springs. Exhausted as he was by drudgery and misfortune, that man was the first Arzamasian who dared to make my acquaintance. The wise Arzamasian authorities had most strictly forbidden the employees of the Zemstvo and all other civil servants to visit me, and, in order to intimidate them, had established a police post just under my windows.

Father Feodor came to me one evening, in pouring rain, soaking wet from head to foot, soiled with clay, in heavy peasant boots, in a grey cassock, and in a faded hat—it was so wet that it looked like a lump

---

[1] Gorky was forbidden to reside in any of the large towns of Russia, and as punishment for his political views was exiled by the authorities to the remote provincial town of Arzamas.

of soaked clay. Pressing my hand tightly with his horny, digger's hand he said, in a stern little bass voice:

"Are you the unrepentant sinner who has been foisted on us for the good of your soul ? We will do your soul good! Can you treat me to tea ? "

In his grey little beard the dried-up little face of an ascetic was hidden. From his deep sockets shone the meek smile of understanding eyes.

"I have come straight from the forest. Have you got any garments into which I could change ? "

I had already heard a great deal about him. I knew that his son was a political exile, one daughter was in prison " for politics," a second daughter was intent on her preparations to get there. I knew that he had already spent all his means on this search for water, had mortgaged his house, and was now living like a pauper, himself digging ditches in the forest and stopping them with clay. When his strength failed he would implore the neighbouring peasants, for the love of Christ, to lend him a hand. They would help him; but the townspeople, sceptically watching the work of this " queer " parson, would not lift a finger.

It was this man whom Leonid Andreev met at my house.

It was October, a dry cold day, the wind was

blowing; in the streets scraps of paper, birds' feathers and onion peels were flying about. The dust scratched against the window-panes, a huge rain-cloud moved from the fields to the town. Suddenly, into our room came Father Feodor, rubbing his dust-covered eyes, shaggy, angry, cursing the thief who had stolen his handbag and umbrella, and the Governor-General, who refused to understand that a water supply is more useful than a credit bank. Leonid opened his eyes wide, and whispered to me:

" What is this ? "

An hour later, at the samovar, with his mouth quite agape, he listened to the archpriest of the absurd town of Arzamas denouncing the Gnostics for having fought against the democratic principles of the Church and for trying to make instruction in the knowledge of God inaccessible to the minds of the people.

" These heretics consider themselves seekers after the highest knowledge, aristocrats of the spirit. But are not the people, in the persons of their wisest guides, the embodiment of the wisdom of God and of His spirit ?

" ' Docetists,' ' Ophites,' ' Pleroma,' ' Carpocrates,' "
—Father Feodor droned on, and Leonid, nudging me with his elbow, whispered:

" There is the Arzamasian horror incarnate! "

But soon he was waving his hand in front of Father
Feodor's face as he proved to him the impotence of
thought; and the priest, shaking his beard, retorted:
" It is not thought that is impotent, but unbelief."
" But that is the essence of thought. . . ."
" You are sophisticated, Mr. Author. . . ."
The rain lashed the window-panes, the old man
and the young one rummaged among ancient
wisdom, and from the wall Leo Tolstoy, with the
little stick in his hand—the great pilgrim of this
world—gazed down on them. Having overthrown
everything we could in the time, we went to our rooms
long after midnight. I was already in bed, with a
book, when there came a knock at my door and
Leonid appeared, dishevelled, agitated, his shirt
collar undone, he sat down on my bed and began
rapturously:
" What a parson! How he found me out, eh ? "
And suddenly tears gleamed in his eyes.
" Lucky fellow you, Alexei, the devil take you.
You always have wonderfully interesting people
round you, and I—am lonely . . . or I have hanging
on to me. . . ."
He waved his hand. I began telling him of the life
of Father Feodor, how he had been seeking for water;
of the book he had written, *The History of the Old
Testament*, the MS. of which had been taken away

from him by order of the Synod; of his book *Love the Law of Life*, also forbidden by the ecclesiastical censorship. In that book Father Feodor proved by quotations from Pushkin and from other poets that the feeling of love, as between one man and another, was the basis of life and of the progress of the world, that it was as powerful as the law of universal gravitation, and resembled it in every respect.

" Yes," said Leonid musingly, " there are things I must learn; otherwise I feel ashamed before the parson. . . ."

Another knock at the door. Enter Father Feodor, folding his cassock round him, barefooted, sad.

" You are not asleep ? So, well. . . . Here I am! I heard talking, I thought I'd come and apologize! I rather shouted, young people, but don't take offence. . . . I lay down, thought of you. You are nice people. I decided that I had grown warm for no reason. . . . Now, here I am, forgive me! I'm going to bed. . . ."

Both sat down on the bed, and again began an endless conversation. Leonid, elated, laughed again and again.

" What a country this Russia of ours is! ' Look here, we haven't yet solved the problem of the existence of God, and you are calling us to dinner! ' It is not Byelinsky who says this, it is what all Russia says to Europe. For Europe, in the main, calls us to dine, to feed well, nothing but this!"

And Father Feodor, wrapping his thin, bony legs in his cassock, smilingly replied:

"After all, Europe is our godmother, don't forget it! Without her Voltaires, without her men of science, we should not now be disputing about matters philosophical, but should be silently swallowing *bleeny* [pancakes]—and only that!"

At daybreak Father Feodor left us, and in a couple of hours he was gone—to set about work again on the Arzamasian water supply. And Leonid having slept till evening, said to me then:

"Just think, in whose interest and for what purpose is it that in this rotten little town a parson should live who is energetic, interesting and a wizard? And why indeed should the parson of this town be a wizard, eh? What nonsense? You know one can live only in Moscow. Come, leave this place. It is horrid here —rain, dirt. . . ."

And immediately he began preparing to go home. At the railway station he said:

"And yet this parson is an oddity. It is all a story!"

He complained more than once that he scarcely met any big, original people:

"Now, you can find them; while only burrs that I drag along on my tail stick to me. Why is it?"

I mentioned people whose acquaintance would be useful to him—men of high culture or of original mind. I spoke to him of V. V. Rozanov and others. It seemed to me that an acquaintance with Rozanov would be extremely useful to Andreev. He was surprised!

" I can't make you out! "

And he spoke of Rozanov's conservatism, which he need not have done, since his essential self was profoundly indifferent to politics, only now and then displaying fits of external curiosity about them. His real attitude to political activities he expressed most sincerely in his story *As it was—So it will be.*

I tried to prove to him that one can learn from the devil himself or a thief as well as from a saintly recluse, and that study does not mean submission.

" That is not quite true," he replied, " all learning represents submission to facts. And Rozanov I don't like. He reminds me of the dog in the Bible who returns to his vomit."

At times it seemed as if he avoided personal acquaintance with big people because he was afraid of their influence on him. He would meet such a person once or twice. Sometimes he would praise him ardently; but his interest was short-lived.

So it was with Savva Morosov. After the first long conversation with him, Andreev, carried away by the man's subtle mind, wide knowledge and energy, called him Yermak Timofeevich (the conqueror of Siberia), and said that he would play a great political role:

" He has the face of a Tartar; but, my dear fellow, he is an English lord! "

And Savva Morosov said of Andreev:

" He only appears self-assured; but he does not feel confidence in himself and seeks to obtain it from his mind. But his mind wavers. He knows that and does not trust it. . . ."

§

I write as my memory prompts me, with no care for sequence or for chronology.

In the Moscow Art Theatre, when it was still in Karetni Row, Leonid introduced me to his fiancee, a slim, fragile girl with lovely clear eyes. Modest, reserved, she appeared to me unoriginal; but I soon became convinced that she was a person of an understanding heart.

She realized splendidly the need of a maternal, watchful attitude to Andreev, at once and deeply she comprehended the significance of his talent and the tormenting fluctuations of his mood. She was one of those rare women who, capable of being passionate mistresses, are yet able to love with the love of a mother. This double love armed her with a subtle knowledge, so that she had a marvellous understanding of the genuine complainings of his soul as well as of the high-sounding words of a capricious passing mood.

As is known, a Russian " For a word that is witty shows his father and mother no pity," Leonid, too, was very much carried away by words that were " witty," and at times composed maxims in very dubious taste.

" A year after marriage a wife is like a well-worn boot: one does not feel it," he said once in the presence of Alexandra Mikhailovna (his wife). She was capable of taking no notice of such phrase-making, and at times even found these pranks of the tongue witty, and laughed caressingly. But, possessing a strong sense of self-respect, she could—if need be—show herself very obstinate, even immovable. There was subtly developed in her a taste for the music of words, for forms of speech. She was small, lithe, elegant, and at times somewhat amusingly, childishly grave—I nicknamed her " Lady Shura "[1] —the name stuck to her.

Leonid valued her, and she lived in constant concern for him, in a continuous tension of all her

[1] " Shura " is the diminutive pet form of " Alexandra."

powers, her personality was completely sacrificed to her husband's interests.

At the Andreevs' house in Moscow authors often met together, it was very crowded and cosy. "Lady Shura's" lovely eyes, smiling caressingly, restrained to a certain extent the "breadth" of Russian natures. Chaliapin often put in an appearance, fascinating everyone with his stories.

When "Modernism" was in full flower an attempt was made at the Andreev gatherings to understand it. But on the whole it was condemned, which was much the simplest way. There was no time to think seriously of literature; war and politics were of first importance. Blok, Byely, Bryussov, appeared "isolated provincials"; in the most favourable opinion —queer fellows, in the least favourable—something like traitors to "the great traditions of the Russian commonwealth." I also thought and felt like that. Was it the time for a "Symphony" when the whole of Russia was gloomily making ready to dance the *trepak*? Events were moving towards a catastrophe, the symptoms of its approach were becoming ever more and more ominous. The Social Revolutionaries were throwing bombs, and each explosion shook the whole country, calling forth an intense expectation of a fundamental overthrow of social life. It was in Andreev's flat that the sittings of the Central

Committee of the Social Democrats—the Bolsheviks—
took place; and once the whole committee, together
with the host, was arrested and carried off to prison.

Having spent a month in prison Andreev came out
as though from the pool of Siloam—hearty and
cheerful.

" It does one good to be tied down," he said, "it
makes you want to fly out in all directions! "

And he laughed at me.

" Well, now, pessimist. Is not Russia coming to
life ? And you rhymed: ' autocracy—gone rusty.' "

He published then his stories *The Marseillaise, The
Alarm, The Story which will never be finished.* But already
in October 1905 he read to me the MS. of his story
As it was.

" Is it not premature ? " I asked.

" The good is always premature . . ." he answered.

Soon he went off to Finland and was right in doing
so: the senseless brutality of the December events
would have crushed him. In Finland he was active
politically; he spoke at meetings, published in
Helsingfors papers bitter attacks on the policy of the
Monarchists. But his mood was depressed, his view
on the future hopeless. In Petersburg I received a
letter from him. Among other things he wrote:

" Each horse has its inborn peculiarities, nations,
too. There are horses for which all roads lead to the

public-house: our country is now turned towards a
goal most beloved by it and for a long time it will go
on in a drunken frenzy."

§

A few months later we met in Switzerland, at
Montreux. Leonid jeered at the life of the Swiss:

" We people of large plains can't live in these cockroach holes," he would say.

It appeared to me he had become somewhat faded,
dimmed; a glassy expression of fatigue and of dis-
quieting sadness showed in his eyes. Of Switzerland he
spoke as flatly, as superficially, and in the same words
as the freedom-loving inhabitants of Chukhloma,
Konotop and Tetiushi have been wont to speak for
ever so long. One of these defined the Russian notion
of freedom profoundly and pointedly in these words:

" In our town we live as in a public bath, without
restrictions, without ceremony."

About Russia Leonid spoke reluctantly and
tediously, and once sitting by the fireplace he recalled
a few lines of Yakubovich's melancholy poem " To
My Country."

> Why should we love thee,
> Art thou our mother?

" I have written a play. Shall we read it ? "

And in the evening he read *Savva*.

While he was still in Russia, hearing about young Ufimtsev and his comrades, who attempted to blow up the icon of the Virgin of Kursk, Andreev decided to work this episode into a story, and at that very time he at once created the plan of the story and definitely outlined the characters. He was particularly fascinated by Ufimtsev, a poet in the domain of scientific technique, a youth who possessed the undoubted talent of an inventor. Exiled to the Semiretchensk province, I believe to Karkarali, living there under the strict surveillance of men ignorant and superstitious, who denied him the necessary tools and materials, he invented an original motor of internal combustion, perfected the cyclostyle, worked on a new system of dredging, invented a " permanent cartridge " for sporting guns. I showed the designs of his motor to engineers at Moscow, and they told me that Ufimtsev's invention was very practical, ingenious and clever. I don't know the fate of all these inventions—having settled abroad I lost sight of Ufimtsev.

But I knew that young man was one of those superb dreamers who, carried away by their belief and love, march in different ways to one and the same goal—the arousing in their people of that sensible energy that creates goodness and beauty.

I was sad and vexed to see that Andreev had distorted such a character, as yet untouched in Russian
literature. It seemed to me that in the story, in the
way it had been conceived, that character should
have found the appreciation and the tone worthy of
it. We had a little argument, and perhaps I spoke
rather sharply of the necessity of representing
exactly certain—most rare and positive—pheno-
mena of actuality.

Like all people of a definitely circumscribed
" ego," with a keen perception of their " selfness,"
Leonid did not like being contradicted. He took
offence, and we parted coldly.

§

I believe it was in 1907 or 1908 that Andreev
arrived at Capri, after burying " Lady Shura " in
Berlin—she died of puerperal fever. The death of
this sensible and good friend reacted very painfully
on Leonid's soul. All his thoughts and words centred
in recollections of the senselessness of it.

" You understand," he said, with strangely dilated
pupils, " she was still alive as she lay in bed, but
already her breath smelt of a corpse. It was a very
ironical smell."

Dressed in a black velvet jacket he even outwardly

looked crushed, down-trodden. His thoughts and words were weirdly concentrated on the problem of death. It so happened that he settled down in the Villa Caraciollo, which belonged to the widow of an artist, a descendant of the Marquis Caraciollo, that supporter of the French party who had been executed by Ferdinand Bomba. In the dark rooms of that villa it was damp and gloomy; on the walls hung unfinished grimy pictures that looked like mould-stains. In one of the rooms was a large smoke-stained fireplace, and in front of the windows, shading them, grew a dense cluster of shrubs. From the walls of the house ivy crept in at the window-panes. This room Leonid turned into his dining-room.

One evening when I arrived I found him in a chair, in front of the fireplace. Dressed in black and bathed in the purple glow of the smouldering coal, he held on his knees his little son Vadim, and in a low tone, with sobs, was telling him something. I entered softly, it seemed to me that the boy was falling asleep. I sat down on a chair by the door and I heard Leonid telling his son how Death stalked over the earth and mowed down little children.

" I'm frightened," Vadim said.

" Don't you want to hear ? "

" I'm frightened," the boy repeated.

" Well, go to bed. . . ."

M

But the child pressed close to his father's knees and began crying. For long we could not manage to comfort him. Leonid was in a hysterical mood, his words irritated the boy, who stamped his feet and cried:
" I don't want to sleep! I don't want to die! "
When his granny took him away, I observed that it was hardly necessary to frighten the boy with stories like that, stories about Death, the invincible giant.

" But if I can't speak of anything else ? " he said sharply. " At last I understand how indifferent ' beautiful Nature ' is, and I want one thing only—to tear my portrait out of this frivolously pretty frame."

It was difficult, almost impossible, to speak to him. He was nervous, irritable, and it seemed as though he deliberately chafed his wound.

" The idea of suicide haunts me; it seems to me that my shadow crawls after me, whispering ' Begone, die! ' "

This aroused considerable anxiety among his friends; but now and then he would drop hints that he was consciously and deliberately creating this anxiety. It was as though he wished to hear once more what they had to say in justification and defence of life.

But the cheerful scenery of the island, the caressing beauty of the sea, and the genial attitude of the Caprians to the Russians soon drove away Leonid's gloomy mood. In a couple of months he was seized, as by a whirlwind, with a passionate desire for work.

I remember one moonlit night, sitting on the pebbles by the sea, he said, with a shake of his head: "*Basta!* To-morrow morning I'll begin to work!"

"The best thing you could do."

"Just so!"

And—a thing which he had not done for a long time—he began to talk cheerfully of his plans for new books.

"First of all, old fellow, I will write a story with the despotism of friendship for its subject. I'll pay off my score to you, you rascal!"

And instantly he began—easily and quickly—to weave a humorous story of two friends, one a dreamer, the other a mathematician. The one spends his whole life in the clouds, while the other is carefully calculating the expense of these imaginary travels, thereby decidedly killing once and for all the dreams of his friend.

But immediately afterwards he said:

"I want to write about Judas. When I was in Russia I read a poem about him, I don't remember by whom[1]—it was very clever. . . . What do you think of Judas?"

At that time I had a translation of Julius Wexel's

---

[1] By A. Roslavlev.

tetralogy *Judas and Christ*, and a translation of Thor Goedberg's story, also Golovanov's poem. I suggested that he should read them.

" I don't want to, I have an idea of my own, and they might muddle me. You had better tell me what they say. No, you had better not, don't tell me."

As was his way—in moments of creative excitement—he jumped to his feet—he had to move about.

" Let's be off! "

On the way he gave me an account of his *Judas*, and in three days brought me the manuscript. With that story began one of the most productive periods of his creative activity. At Capri he thought out his play *Black Masks*, wrote the caustic satire *Love of One's Neighbour*, the story *Darkness*, created the plan of *Sashka Zheguliov*, sketched out his play *Ocean*, and wrote several chapters—two or three—of his long tale *My Memoirs*—all these in the course of six months. These serious works and plans did not prevent Leonid from taking a lively part in composing the play *Alas!*, a piece in the classical " people's theatre " style, written partly in verse, partly in prose, with songs, dances, and all kinds of tortures perpetrated on the unfortunate Russian peasants. The plot of the play is clearly enough indicated by the list of dramatis personæ:

Oppressum—a merciless landlord.

Furiosa—his wife.

Philisterius—brother to Oppressum, a prose litterateur.

Decadentius—unsuccessful son to Oppressum.

Endurance—a peasant, very unhappy, but not always drunk.

Griefella—Endurance's beloved wife, full of meekness and common sense, although pregnant.

Sufferalla—Endurance's beautiful daughter.

Smackface—a most horrible police-constable (Bathes in full uniform and all his medals).

Mangle—an indubitable village policeman, but, in fact, the noble Count Edmond de Ptié.

Motrya Bell—secretly married to the Count, the Spanish Marchioness Donna Carmen Intolerablia Detestablia, in fact, disguised as a gitana.

The Shadow of the Russian literary critic Skabichevsky.

The Shadow of Koblitz-Yusov.

Athanasius Schapov, in a perfectly sober state.

"We told you so"—a group of persons without words or actions.

The play takes place in " Sky-blue Clay," Oppressum's estate, twice mortgaged to the Noblemen's Bank and once mortgaged somewhere else.

A whole act of this play had been worked out fully saturated with delightful absurdities. Leonid wrote the prose dialogue, which was terribly funny, so droll indeed that he himself laughed like a child at his own inventions.

Never before or since have I seen him in a frame of mind so active, so unusually industrious. He renounced, as it were, for ever, his dislike for the process of writing, and he could sit at his table all day and all night, half-dressed, unkempt, cheerful.

His imagination blazed wonderfully brightly and productively—nearly every day he told me the plan of a new tale or story.

" Now at last I have taken myself in hand," he would say triumphantly.

And he inquired about the famous pirate Barbarossa, about Tommaso Aniello, about smugglers, carbonari, about the life of Calabrian shepherds.

" What a multitude of subjects, what a diversity of life! " He was in raptures.

" Yes, these people have accumulated something for posterity. But with us: I picked up *The Lives of the Russian Tzars*, and read that they ate. I tried to read *The History of the Russian People*—they suffered. I gave it up. The whole thing hurts and bores."

But, while the plans he related were full of colour and substance, he composed carelessly. In the first version of his *Judas* several mistakes occurred which indicated that he had not even taken the trouble to read the New Testament. When he was told that " Duke Spadaro " sounds as absurd to an Italian as " Prince Bashmatchnikov " would to a Russian, and that St. Bernard dogs did not exist in the twelfth century, he was annoyed.

" These are trifles! " he objected.

" One can't say: ' They drink wine like camels,' without adding ' drink water.' "

" Rubbish! " he said.

He behaved to his talent as an indifferent rider treats a superb horse—he galloped it mercilessly, but did not love it, did not tend it. His hand had not the time to draw the intricate designs of his riotous imagination; he did not trouble to develop the power and dexterity of his hand. At moments he himself realized that this was a great hindrance to the normal growth of his talent.

" My language is ossifying. I feel it is getting more difficult for me to find the necessary words. . . ."

He tried to hypnotize the reader by the monotony of his phrasing, but his phrasing was losing the convincing quality of beauty. Wrapping his thought in the cotton wool of monotonously obscure words he only succeeded in revealing it too much, and his stories read like popular dialogues on philosophical subjects.

Now and then, aware of this, he was vexed:

" It is all cobweb, it sticks, but is not solid! Yes, I must read Flaubert. I believe you are right. Indeed he is a descendant of those mason geniuses who built the indestructible temples of the Middle Ages."

§

At Capri Leonid was told an episode of which he made use for his story *Darkness*. The hero of that

episode was an old acquaintance of mine, a revolutionary. In reality, the affair was very simple: a
girl at a brothel, having guessed intuitively that her
visitor was a revolutionary, hunted by detectives and
driven to take shelter there from the pursuit of the
political police, treated him with a mother's tender
care and with the tact of a woman who still possesses
the sense of respect for a hero. But the hero, a bookish
man of clumsy soul, responded to the impulse of the
woman's heart with a sermon on morality, so reminding her of what she wanted to forget at the moment.
Hurt by this she smacked his face—a smack perfectly
deserved, in my opinion. Then, having realized the
whole crudity of his mistake, he apologized to her
and kissed her hand—I think he might have omitted
the kissing. That is all.

Sometimes, unfortunately very seldom, reality
happens to be more truthful and more pleasant than
even a very talented story that is based on it.

So it was in this case. But Leonid distorted the
meaning as well as the form of the event out of
recognition. In the actual brothel there was neither
the agonizing and foul mockery at man, nor even one
of those weird details with which Andreev has
enriched the story so abundantly.

This distortion affected me very painfully: Leonid,
as it were, revoked and annulled the feast which I

had been awaiting long and hungrily. I know people too well not to appreciate—very highly—the least manifestation of a good, honest feeling. Certainly I could not help pointing out to Andreev the meaning of his action, which to me was equivalent to murder for a mere whim, for a wicked whim. He reminded me of the freedom of the artist, but this did not change my attitude—even now I am not convinced that such rare manifestations of ideally human feelings should be arbitrarily distorted by the artist, for the gratification of a dogma he loves.

We talked long on this theme. But although our conversation bore a perfectly peaceful friendly character, still from that moment something snapped between me and him.

The end of that conversation is very memorable to me:

"What are you trying for?" I asked Leonid.

"I don't know," he said, shrugging his shoulders and closing his eyes.

"But you certainly have some desire—either it is always there before all others, or it arises more often than all others?"

"I don't know," he repeated. "I believe there is nothing of the sort. Sometimes, though, I feel that I need fame—much fame, as much as the whole world could give. Then I concentrate it in myself,

condense it to its ultimate capacity, and when it has
acquired the force of explosive matter, I explode,
illuminating the world with a new light. And after
that people will begin to live with a new mind. You
see, what we need is a new mind, not this lying old
swindler! He takes from me all the best of my flesh,
all my feelings and, promising to return them with
interest, returns nothing, saying: ' To-morrow! '
' Evolution.' Then when my patience is exhausted
and the thirst for life stifles me—' Revolution! ' he
says. And fondly goes on deceiving till I die, having
received nothing."

" You must have belief, not reason."

" Perhaps. But if so, then first of all belief in
myself."

He paced the room in agitation, then sitting down
on the table, waving his hand in front of my face, he
went on:

" I know that God and the Devil are mere symbols.
But it seems to me that the whole life of man, all the
meaning of it, consists in the infinite and boundless
expansion of these symbols, fed with the flesh and
blood of the world. And having invested these two
opposites with all its powers—to the very last—mankind will disappear, but those two will become carnal
realities and will go on living in the emptiness of the
universe, face to face with one another, invincible,

immortal. There is no sense in this. But there is none anywhere, in anything."

He grew pale, his lips trembled, stark terror shone in his eyes. Then he added in a low voice, feebly:

" Let us imagine the Devil as woman, God as man, and let them beget a new being, certainly just as dual as you and I. Just as dual. . . ."

§

He left Capri unexpectedly, all of a sudden. Only the day before his departure he had said to me that he would sit down at his table and work for three months. But on the evening of the very same day he said to me:

" You know, I have decided to leave this place. After all, one must live in Russia. Here one is overcome by a kind of operatic levity—one wants to write vaudevilles—vaudevilles with songs. Life simply is not real here, it is an opera: there is more singing here than thinking. Romeo, Othello and the rest of their kind—Shakespeare made them—the Italians are incapable of tragedy. Here neither Byron nor Poe could have been born."

" And what about Leopardi ? "

" Well, Leopardi, who knows about him ? He is one of those who are talked about, but not read."

As he left he said to me:

" This, Alexeyushko, is also an Arzamas—a gay little Arzamas, no more than that."

" Don't you remember how it fascinated you ? "

" Before marriage we are all fascinated. . . . You will be leaving here soon ? Do go away, it is time you went. You are beginning to look like a monk. . . ."

§

At the time I was living in Italy my mind was very uneasy on account of Russia. As early as 1911 people round me spoke confidently of the inevitability of an all-European war and of the certainty that that war would be fatal to Russians. My uneasy mood was particularly heightened by facts which indicated beyond all doubt that in the spiritual world of the great Russian people there lurked something morbidly obscure. Reading the volume of agrarian risings in the Central Russian provinces, published by the Free Economic Society, I saw that those risings bore a particularly brutal and senseless character. An investigation of the crimes of the population of the Moscow Circuit, based on an examination of the reports of the Moscow High Court, astounded me by its revelation of the tendency of the criminal will, expressed in the great number of cases in crimes against the person, violation of women, and rape of minors. Even before then I had been unpleasantly struck by the fact that, though in the Second State Duma there had been a very considerable number of priests, men of the purest Russian blood, these men had not produced a single talent, a single statesman. And there was a great deal more that confirmed my anxiously sceptical attitude towards the fate of the Great-Russian race.

On my arrival in Finland I met Andreev, and talking to him, told him my cheerless thoughts. Hotly and even as though wounded by them, he argued with me. But his arguments seemed to me unconvincing: he had no facts.

But suddenly, lowering his voice, with his eyes screwed up, as though straining to look into the future, he began to talk of the Russian people in words unusual with him—abruptly, incoherently, and with great and undoubtedly sincere conviction.

I am unable, and if I could I should not like, to reproduce his words. Their force consisted not in their logic nor in their beauty, but in a feeling of tormented sympathy for the people, a feeling of which, in such force and in such expression, I had not thought Leonid capable.

He shook all over with nervous tension, and crying, almost sobbing like a woman, he shouted:

" You call Russian literature provincial because the majority of the great Russian writers are men of the Moscow province ? Good, let us suppose so. But yet it is a world literature, it is the most serious and powerful creative activity of Europe. The genius of Dostoevsky alone is enough in itself to justify even the senseless, even the thoroughly criminal, life of the millions of the people. And suppose the people are spiritually sick—let us heal them and remember as has been said: ' A pearl only grows in a diseased shell.' "

" And the beauty of the beast," I asked.

" And the beauty of human endurance, of meekness and love ? " he replied. And he went on to speak of the people, of literature more and more ardently and passionately.

It was the first time he had spoken so passionately, so lyrically. Previously I had heard such strong expressions of his love applied only to talents congenial to his spirit—to Edgar Poe most frequently of all.

Soon after our conversation the filthy war broke out. Our attitude, different towards it, divided me still further from Andreev. We scarcely met; it was only in 1916, when he brought me his books, that we both once more deeply felt how much we had gone through and what old comrades we were. But, to

avoid arguing, we could speak only of the past;
the present erected between us a high wall of irreconcilable differences.

I shall not be violating the truth if I say that to
me that wall was transparent and permeable—I saw
behind it a big, original man, who for ten years had
been very near to me, my sole friend in literary
circles.

Differences of outlook ought not to affect sym-
pathies, and I never gave theories and opinions a
decisive role in my relations to people.

Leonid Nikolaevich Andreev felt otherwise. But I
don't blame him for this; for he was what he wished
to be and could not help being—a man of rare
originality, rare talent and manly enough in his
seekings after truth.

THE END